# A Strange and Wild Place

*by*

## Sandra Macpherson

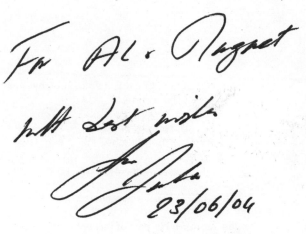

For Al & August

with best wishes

*[signature]*
23/06/04

**Birlinn**

First published in Great Britain in 2004 by
Birlinn Ltd
West Newington House
10 Newington Road
Edinburgh

*www.birlinn.co.uk*

Copyright © Sandra Macpherson, 2004

ISBN 1 84158 286 7

British Library Cataloguing-in-Publication Data
A catalogue record for this book is available on request
from the British Library

Typeset by Initial Typesetting Services
Printed and bound by MPG Books Limited, Bodmin

*For Euan*

# Foreword

I dedicate this book to the memory of my late husband, Euan. He was a man of profound intelligence, a poet, a distinguished writer and above all a gentleman. Euan devoted his life to Glentruim, which he loved so deeply, and with great determination he strove to hold on to his heritage for the sake of generations to come. Without him there would be no story and I thank him for our extraordinary life within his family home.

Our children, Catriona and Lachlan, so much part of us, supported us in our ventures, worked together as a family, united in our quest to save Glentruim. I thank them for this and also for allowing me to write about their stories and strange experiences.

I would like to thank Vicky Thain, my close and longest-standing friend, for her encouragement as she read through draft after draft. Kenneth and Gerry Brown also meticulously read through my manuscript and their comments were immensely helpful, as were those of Rosemary Perkins, whose command of the English language left little room for error as she tirelessly read over page after page. I am very grateful to them all. Also, I would like to thank Sandy Macpherson, with his immense knowledge on Scottish history: he was the source for many dates and events in the Clan Country.

Lastly, a big thank you to all friends mentioned in my book, from the north, throughout Scotland and indeed across the world. With their permission I have related their tales, which gave us such joy then, and more recently when some of us sat together reminiscing. Their memories, my children's and mine form the basis of my book – a span of our lives never to be forgotten and now to be shared by those who read *A Strange and Wild Place*.

# Contents

# North Circuit – Spring 1844

There is a strange wild place called Glen Truim on the left hand (going north), between Dalwhinnie and Kingussie, the progress of which I have been marking since ever it began a few years ago. It is the work of a Major Macpherson, an Indian officer, I believe, who, no doubt from his having run about in a torn kilt here in his youth, has adventured on the rather bold attempt to make a habitable residence in apparently the most savage position of the whole strath. Everybody laughs at him and he has certainly set his mansion too high; but since he has courage to begin, and to live there, I predict its one day being a fine and not uncomfortable highland place. It will depend entirely on the wood he will be able to coax into life.

*Circuit Journeys* by the late Lord Cockburn (1975)

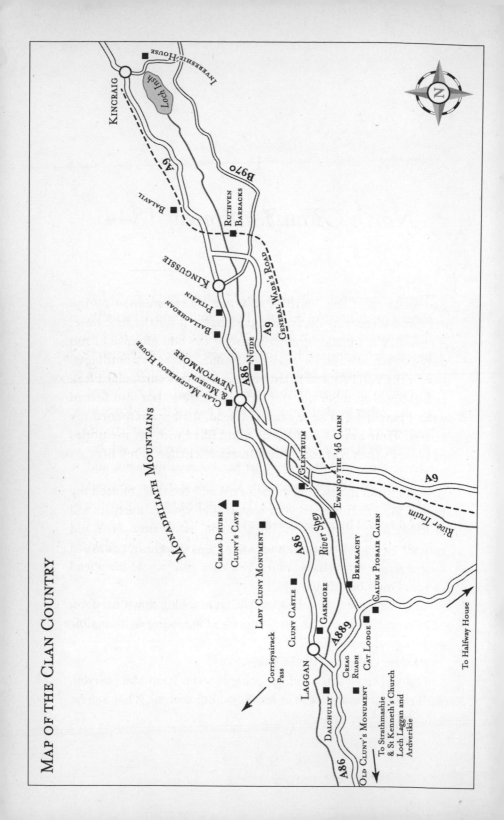

# Map of the Clan Country

# 1

# *The Journey*

I never tired of this journey, and was always stunned by the dramatic scenery as if I were experiencing it for the first time. As usual, I scanned the mountains for the odd glimpse of red deer, which would be scarcely visible, being camouflaged within the bracken and faded heather. On this particular bleak and chilly November day not only excitement, but also fear of what I perceived to be my future ahead, further sharpened my senses. Time passed swiftly, my mind filled with the memories of events which had led to this dramatic change in my life.

'Do you mean the chap with the beard and sandals?' blurted my father. 'He's twenty years your senior. When you're thirty he will be fifty, and, when you're fifty he will be seventy. He's old enough to be your father, and, anyway, you have not finished your training yet. What is more, you have your whole life ahead of you. Don't be ridiculous!'

'But I love him', I replied weakly, tears rolling down my face, as I sat on the floor at his feet, future and age being so intangible at the age of twenty-one.

We were the talk of the Hospital.

'Did you know that Sandra is going out with Euan Macpherson, the Principal Psychologist at the Royal Edinburgh? What a great catch he will be,' some said.

'There is quite an age gap, isn't there?' others remarked, and 'I believe she is one of his students!' – What scandal!

Well, we did get married, in 1968, on my twenty-second birthday and it was a very happy occasion, with 200 guests in all. I could not remember being so happy, and marriage to Euan was a very precious gift as far as I was concerned, despite beard, sandals and age. What I did not know in those early days was what was to come with this marriage – the extraordinary inheritance. Not all were worldly goods; there was history and the unexplained.

Euan had often reminded me of the time we first met, in my nursing days. I had hung my coat on his coat rack, while attending one of his talks in his office, and he said that he loved its smell! He had also told me that I was exceedingly inattentive, my mind drifting as always on something else. I was more mesmerised by his deep hypnotic voice, his way with words and, of course, his extremely good looks. His carefully groomed beard was red, such a contrast to his dark brown hair and eyes to match – the eyes of a true Macpherson. These eyes appeared to read your mind, so befitting of a psychologist. With all these attributes and when in full Highland regalia, he was quite the Highland chieftain.

I was invited on my first date with Euan, following a training afternoon in his department, and it was to be for a meal at Prestonfield House in Edinburgh. My flat-mates and I had stayed behind after the lecture, individually carrying out personality tests. We were in separate rooms; when I had finished I could not believe that my friends had already completed theirs and gone home with their results. When I asked Euan if I could wait for the result of mine, he said, 'It is late now, but I shall give them to you over dinner tomorrow night!'

That next evening my colleagues hung out of the windows of the nurses' home, from where Euan was picking me up, to watch me go off – mainly to have a glimpse of our tutor! Wearing the kilt, Euan looked extremely dashing, and I have to admit I was the envy of all of my year that night, when he got out of his car to open my door. That was a different world for me then.

The Highlands of Scotland have indeed incredibly beautiful places, some secret yet also forebidding! Our destination was no exception. Oh yes, there was the beauty and the tranquillity, but is there not always a price to pay?

'Not far now,' I remember Euan saying, gently placing his hand on my knee, which had to be carefully manoeuvred under Crubie, my sheltie, a blanket of warmth and truly welcome on such a day. I had had him since he was a pup and he had become a constant companion to me during my recent troublesome pregnancy. We had almost given up hope of a child since my miscarriage the year after we married, but two years further on I was pregnant again – a joyous realization marred only by its timing, which was to take me away from our home outside Edinburgh, to deal with a pre-planned commitment. It was the second time that I had been asked to look after Euan's old Aunt Katie, who lived at Glentruim.

The first time I went north to look after Aunt Katie had been for the same reason, which was to enable her housekeeper to get away for a break. I received a terrible reception. The housekeeper took an instant dislike to me and was determined to undermine me from the start. The dear old aunt, however, welcomed me with open arms and I felt drawn to her by her sorrow and loneliness. She too, as she had confided in me, had suffered a miscarriage, but sadly it was her only pregnancy. After the death of her husband she had no one to share her huge pile of a home with, and to me her life was utterly tragic.

Glentruim was a mausoleum, caught in a time-warp. Though furnished with spectacular antiques, its elegance had faded, its fabrics were outworn and its décor was of the previous century. The housekeeper enforced rigid routines, where everything happened by the stroke of the clock. Even the shopping went by the rule. The weekly food provisions arrived every Saturday when the butcher delivered one small chicken (roast for Sunday), one pound of sausages and one pound of mince. I had strict instructions as to when and how these rations were to be cooked. There was no refrigerator, only an old lean-to larder with slate slabs, meat-hooks on the ceiling and mesh covers for the food. Fortunately vegetables were plentiful, straight from the garden, and could supplement the meagre order very nicely.

On the second visit, the housekeeper informed me that she would stay one night, before leaving for her holiday, only to give out instructions on the daily routine, which on no account should be altered. Euan, thankfully, planned to stay for a couple of days before returning early Monday morning for his work in Edinburgh. I was also to have the pleasure of looking after the ferocious little Scottish terrier. He, too, had taken a dislike to me and never missed an opportunity to nip me on the ankle. Intimidating as the housekeeper was, I was actually grateful that she was to stay the first night. Euan's aunt, who was by then bedridden, looked very poorly. Alas, she was very ill and died during that very first night. Was I glad of her unwelcoming companion! I knew immediately when I heard the high-pitched shriek around dusk, calling for 'Master Euan'. The housekeeper's voice echoed through the whole building, the very walls answering her cry. The shock was bad enough for me in my condition, but the thought of it happening had I been alone and in charge was horrifying.

Blood relatives came from near and far. After her death those who previously could not possibly have come to look after Aunt Katie flew in, like bees to a honey pot, and were all comfortably ensconced by the afternoon of the next day. They seemed to be from the same mould as the housekeeper, with whom they were thick as thieves. Needless to say, I felt that they also disliked me, perhaps because I was to be the future Lady of Glentruim, my husband being the direct male descendant of the family. In their opinion I was far too young to be the next mistress of the house; youth can be such an enemy to those who have lost it.

I was stricken with grief at the loss of such a lovely lady, having got to know Katie well when I had looked after her before. I loved cooking and thus, ignoring the instructions of the housekeeper, had given Katie new and interesting meals, which were enjoyed thoroughly with no adverse affect. Her routine also had been totally disrupted as we chatted and laughed together, passing the days as we pleased and ignoring the time of the clock, also with no adverse affect. The house-dog was the only hindrance; at times a sharp kick was the only way to avoid contact with the old teeth and menacing growls in order to reach his mistress. During that time I learnt of her joys, her heartbreaks and of the power a particular nephew of hers had over her. He was her advisor and held the purse strings. How she would have loved a new carpet in her bedroom, she told me with tears in her eyes, but her request was refused. The carpet was a disaster waiting to happen, worn away to holes by many years of pacing the floor, perhaps in anguish of the hard hand of life. Who knows? A new car she also longed for, but hoped in vain. She was a proud lady who kept herself well groomed and as smart as her wardrobe would allow. I was always struck by the way she kept all of the hair from her brush to place in a thin hairnet as a cover for her head, cruelly depleted of hair by age. Being persuaded that she had only just enough money to live on, she lived frugally, and even the heating barely kept off the chill. The elderly have enough fixations regarding lack of finance without it being reinforced and, surprisingly, there was an abundance left at the end of her life.

During that fatal last visit, never was there such busyness in a supposedly grieving family. Euan and I quietly watched as bureau after bureau was opened and shut, documents were scrutinised and memorised, and personal effects were rummaged through with no respect. I watched until I could bear it no longer, and dared to hint that nothing should be touched until the lawyers arrived. This comment was treated with great contempt, as indeed was I. Emotions, vulnerability and youth were certainly attributes to my disadvantage and not to this day have I ever felt so helpless. Dining all together in silence every evening was crucifying. There was a rush to sit at the head of the table until Euan firmly stated that this seat should remain empty until after the reading of the will.

It was a warm August day when the funeral took place. A solemn time, added to which came even more unrest. It had been decided that family flowers would be placed on top of the coffin, before the journey up to the family graveyard at the top of the torr. Our flowers had arrived, but those of Aunt Katie's blood relatives had not. An extremely disrespectful scene followed. We were told to remove our wreath, but I firmly insisted that it would remain. Lack of confidence, mixed with fury, shook my whole body; I felt wretched. The chosen men placed the coffin on their shoulders and then, as was traditional, we followed on foot behind the coffin, which was preceded by the piper. A slow, melancholy journey, marching in time to the sound of the pipes up to the torr, brought us to the Glentruims' resting-place. Local Macphersons and close friends attended and it was a fairly small funeral, easily catered for afterwards with the usual dram and sandwiches in the Glentruim dining room.

We were not permitted to stay for long, not being executors of the will. As soon as the funeral was over and the will read we were turned out of this home which Euan had by then inherited from his ancestors. The large front doors were opened wide and then closed firmly behind us to conceal the 'looting and raking'.

'I'll give you a year at the utmost' was the remark barely heard on departure, spat between the teeth of Katie's nephew, like the old terrier with his growl.

Because of my pregnancy, we did not travel back to Edinburgh that night but stayed in another grand Macpherson house near Kingussie. It was there that I acquired my sheltie. He was only a few weeks old at the time and looked just like a little white powder puff. We called him Crubenmore, after a place on Glentruim, which was quickly shortened to Crubie.

We were given five years, according to the will, to keep Glentruim solvent and manage the estate. If we had to sell within that time, then our inheritance was to be signed over to the other side of the family. The executors took months to process the will and only when they had completely finished were we allowed to return to our rightful heritage. There was no money in the will for us, only vast quantities of land, numerous farms and buildings and enormous overheads, with very little income. For the sake of Euan's ancestors we were determined to hold on to this family home, considering it to be a lifelong challenge, which was compounded by the added burden of death duties.

We reached the little gate lodge at the foot of the long avenue of trees and began the trail up to Glentruim. Branches hung from both sides as if to both capture and cocoon us in our new abode. I could feel my pulse quicken with anticipation as I recalled my words to Euan on my very first visit, 'An enchanting place, but please don't ever ask me to live here alone.' This was precisely what was in front of me, since Euan's job in Edinburgh would keep us apart for at least a year. Crubie gave a slight shiver as he woke, sensing the change of road surface together with the change in my mood.

It lightened as we left the last of the trees and there, before us, stood the overwhelming granite building, its tower peering over us as if inspecting the new arrivals before allowing their entry.

The crunching of the gravel came simultaneously with the awe-inspiring views over the valley directly below the mansion, reaching far beyond its immaculate terraced lawns, flanked by neatly-pruned yew trees. The view was soon gone as we pulled up on the other side by the large oak door, over which the family crest proudly presided.

'Here we are, we have arrived,' I clearly remember Euan uttering, through a deep sigh. I took in the vastness of the whole place, the steep banks looking onto the front door, the old Wellingtonia trees and others of numerous varieties at the top, with their thick trunks and height that pierced the skies. The pathways and drive continued beyond the Big House, on to many of the retainers' cottages, once again passing views of spacious countryside.

Truim, Euan's black labrador, bounded out of the back of the car, thrilled with the space, tail wagging frantically as his nose disappeared into one rabbit hole after another. My sheltie, not so bold, explored a little before returning to my side. Euan took my arm as we approached the door, its brass doorknob gleaming brightly. He then pulled the equally shiny old doorbell. After a few seconds, we could hear in the distance its long tailored peal, and then, as we silently waited, we heard sharp little footsteps gradually getting louder as they reached the other side of the door which hid our new world.

# 2

# *Behind Closed Doors*

THE door was furtively opened by Miss Sparrow, the housekeeper, the name well suited to her tiny frame and frail physique. 'The Sparrow', as we later referred to her, beckoned us in, addressing her words only to Euan with not even a glance thrown in my direction.

'Come away in, Master Euan,' her voice crooned in a shrill, sing-song fashion, as if to muffle inner smirks. Bent with age, her eyes rarely met ours, but if they did they were rather those of a hawk than a sparrow, the thick-rimmed spectacles magnifying a quizzing intrusive glare. Her white hair was pulled into a neat little bun at the back of her bowed head, while scrawny hands wrung before her as if anticipating some prey. She was a fearsome image as she showed us in.

Our reception was as icy as the house itself. The chill inside matched that outdoors and the smell was, just as I had remembered, of musty damp and old, old things. Stags' heads looked down on me from all sides, and birds of prey, perched on plinths, sat with smaller birds beneath their talons. It was dark and dingy; a single bulb with no shade gave little light over the dark oak table and chairs in the middle of the hall and the matching bookcase against the wall. Grand portraits of ancestors looked down on the thick, shiny linoleum covering the floor, which had been highly polished to catch their reflection, given more light of day. It was sparse, this great hall, not at all as it had been in days gone by.

Silence reigned as Euan opened door after door to find emptiness. The drawing-room empty, no furniture, no carpet, no lightshade, only the magnificent gilt mirror over the marble mantlepiece. The boudoir, empty. Dining-room empty except for a sideboard. Kitchen, almost bare, with a rusty old cooker, a dresser which had seen better days, an inadequate kitchen table and a rickety armchair. Thankfully, some of the bedrooms had a little furniture, beds being the most important, but the executors of the will, like leeches, had almost bled the place dry.

And so it went on until we came to the smoking-room. This panelled room was unchanged and had remained so for the last century; the furniture stood fast as if to defy any living soul to disturb its ways.

I so clearly remember the conversation that followed, which will remain with me always.

'No, Master Euan, your wife cannot enter here,' The Sparrow's authoritative voice distinctly ordered, 'no woman was ever allowed to put a foot in the smoking-room.'

'About time they did, and this will be the first of many changes,' Euan retorted angrily, leading the way.

'Why is there no heating, Miss Sparrow? The place is freezing.'

'No oil in the tanks, Master Euan. Shall I light the paraffin fire?'

'Yes, and I will light the open fire.'

'That fire has not been lit for over fifty years, you can't do that.'

'Yes I can, and what's more I will, Miss Sparrow.'

While The Sparrow busied herself in pursuit of paraffin for the inadequate heater, Euan took himself off to the woodshed to bring in fuel for the open fire. The woodshed was bare, so he ventured out into the woods to gather manageable lengths, and therefore some time passed before he returned.

Tired from the journey and chilled to the marrow, I numbly dropped numbly into the nearest easy chair, my outdoor clothes drawn closer around me. I hardly noticed the scurrying of The Sparrow as she replenished the paraffin heater, but I knew it was lit when the distinctive fumes filled the air. Tears filled my eyes but, blinking furiously, I was determined not to lose face in front of her. No, she would not have the satisfaction of deflating me so early in her game. Women *had* been in this room before; had she chosen to forget their presence in this very room at the reading of the will?

The lawyer reading the will sat where I sat now, I recalled. Euan's cousin by marriage, who had held the purse strings, sat opposite. Euan and I sat together on the couch with another cousin, and her daughter sat behind us on an upright chair. The 'uninvited guest' as 'The Cousin' so eloquently described him, our lawyer, sat on Euan's other side. Everyone had played his or her part well, for you do not have to be able to act to be on a stage such as this. The masks of respect fitted the beneficiaries perfectly, their lines well rehearsed. When the curtain came down after this performance, hands were shaken and we went our different ways, never to meet again.

In came Euan, now warmed from the exertion of chopping. The wood was wet and required encouragement from paper spills dipped in paraffin, but even then the fire was reluctant to start, spluttering and sparking as sap and water trickled down into the grate. This large black fireplace with matching marble mantlepiece and surrounds was my favourite in the house. Cannon balls from the Peninsular War sat on the tiled surfaces either side of the grate and over the top were brass figures, tinder-boxes and a square marble clock. The two very impressive candlesticks made with cannon balls from the Siege of Paris at each end of this mantelpiece were worthy topics of conversation. Euan had by then taken the scuffed bellows from where they normally hung on the bell-pull, and tried to coax the stubborn fire into giving us a little warmth. Coal might have helped but the large brass coal-box only stored newspapers, coal being rarely used since wood was so plentiful on the estate. The fire was struggling, the wood far too wet; it smoked profoundly and then began to flag, as did I.

Our bags had already been taken upstairs, so I left Euan to his tedious task and decided to go to our room and start unpacking. The bedroom we were to have was sparsely furnished, but its saving grace was its glorious views across the valley.

Were we not expected? The beds were unmade, bare and cold. I searched for clean linen and blankets, then, once the beds were made, found two old stone bottles to fill and place under the covers. Damp, I thought as I saw steam rise, accompanied by that tell-tale smell. The Sparrow had no welcome in her heart. Familiar objects, however, lightened my spirits as I carefully placed my belongings around me. A little bit of home!

'How will I cope,' I thought to myself, 'once Euan has gone back to Edinburgh? How do you converse with someone who does not acknowledge you and how can you run a place without conversing?' So few pieces of furniture! Tears rolled down my cheeks. Fatigue, pregnancy and disappointment had taken their toll.

Back downstairs, the temperature in the smoking-room having comfortably risen, only then did I take off my coat; The Sparrow had donned hers and was now at the door bidding us goodnight.

'Are you going out?' Euan had questioned, startled by her attire. Darkness had fallen and with it had come the snow.

'Well, I'm not staying here,' was her reply, 'I am going to my cottage.'

She had been left, in the will, life rent of the first cottage up the drive, 'Piper's Cottage'.

'Where are the two housemaids?' Euan had asked sharply, presuming, as did I, that she herself would be back as usual in the morning.

'Oh, they have gone to the village, Master Euan. Like me, they wouldn't stay when they knew *she* was coming, oh no no,' she had twittered – she always twittered.

I was shaken by her answer: the girls had never known me. Miss Sparrow did not even look my way. I was ignored. She intimated that a cold supper tray was on the hall table and that she would be back in the morning, only to show us how to work the boiler; then she would be on her way.

Euan reassured me, as we veered towards the warmth again, that he would send for Carr in the morning to go and fetch the girls. Carr was the chauffeur, a charming gentleman with the Highland lilt in his voice; he had been with the family for very many years and in his younger days had been gamekeeper. We sat by the fire that night for a short time after our cold supper and I marvelled at this room. It certainly had stood still – you could feel the past. The shelves along one side of the room were packed with books all leather-bound and inside endorsed with the family crest. I could visualise the gentlemen of days gone by sitting here with their pipes, sipping their drams and exchanging long tales. Through the closet door at the far end of the room was the 'Laird's Loo'. In here was a toilet, with a thick mahogany seat, and from the tank, high up on the wall, hung a long metal chain with a porcelain handle at the end. The small basin immediately opposite the toilet however, only supplied water from the cold tap. The smoking-room was indeed a room of all conveniences for the gentlemen after dinner!

Probably the most ornate picture frame I have ever seen sur- rounding a print, of Prince Charlie riding down the Royal Mile in Edinburgh, took up almost one half of a wall in the smoking- room. The carvings on the oak frame were incredible, a figure of a Macpherson on the left side and a MacDonald on the right, both in Highland dress and standing over a foot high. Also around the frame were harps, bagpipes and weapons of all sorts. Other pictures in the room depicted clansmen and well-known scenes of stags such as 'The Monarch of the Glen'. There were also two large desks, one with a roll top, a large oval table, a couch and several exceedingly comfortable armchairs, yet still there was space. While the gentlemen revelled in this large room for many an hour, the ladies would have been in the drawing-room having a more genteel evening. I suspect they would be picking up their needlework while engaging in light chit-chat. Euan had once told me that his Uncle Duncan, Katie's late husband, often used say to him, when he was a little boy, 'Women are such kittle cattle, how they love their tittle tattle.' What a haven the smoking-room must have been for him then!

True to her word The Sparrow was back the next morning and true to her word she left that day, to shut herself in Piper's Cottage and sever all connections with the 'Big House'. Because we were shown the oddities necessary to run the place, the bare essentials only, much would have to be learned by trial and error. Thankfully, the Scottish terrier went with her, but did not leave without making his presence felt, having tried to take on both of our dogs at the same time. Sparks flew as we held them back, their paws frantically skating beneath them on the polished hall floor, barks and growls offending our ears.

Fortunately, basic furniture equipped the servants' quarters, and the girls were brought back to work their notice. Alas, they could not stay with us for long; they were from New Zealand and their visas were running out. The Sparrow had painted a harsh picture of me to them, I later found out, so that I did not blame them for absconding before our arrival. They were about my age and intuitively sensed that I had to deal with a difficult situation. Many a night when they went out I could see that they felt pity for me being alone, pregnant and in a strange place.

Euan stayed only a few days and did his best to make me as comfortable as possible. The log-baskets were filled and extra wood was stored in the woodshed. A newly-purchased freezer was stocked and provisions brought in from the village to last the week, to be replenished at the weekends when Euan returned. As The Sparrow had also been left the estate car, I did not have a car of my own and hence had to rely on the retired estate-workers for fetching any emergency shopping from Newtonmore three miles away.

When Euan left after the first weekend I felt as frightened as an unwanted pup, given as a present and later to be abandoned once the novelty wore off. I stood on the doorstep early that Monday morning and watched him drive off down the avenue. I watched until the car went around the corner and out of sight, trembling with the thought of what was in store for me, and with the raw bite in the winter air. The dogs were my only solace and I was thankful for their companionship. It was an extremely hard time for me, no soul-mate, no friends, and a difficult place to heat in which I rattled around, all alone.

I had never run a household before, let alone such a grand and distinguished one. I felt that I should be well presented at all times, even first thing in the morning, when morning sickness, which continued throughout my pregnancy, made me feel so wretched. It was an effort to get up each day, looking the part, even though I might see no-one except the girls. I kept my long black hair meticulously groomed and if anyone had to be reprimanded then it was piled up high on top of my head, to give me stature. Youth and inexperience could never be hidden and this was always to my disadvantage in those early days.

The new young gardener, whom I saw walking up the avenue each morning, would disappear into the potting shed at the bottom of the vegetable garden for the rest of the day. Being winter, he knew better than I what jobs had to be undertaken and I trustingly left him to it. I rarely saw Carr, but from time to time he drove his wife past the house to go shopping. I was curious as to why they came down our drive – the retainers' drive was just as quick – but of course there was a gate to open! Kennedy, the retired gardener, never ventured out of his cottage, but loved a visit to relate stories of himself and the late Laird. The retainer who lived in the cottage beside his, had already set plans in motion to go and stay with relatives because of his advanced years. As for The Sparrow, if by chance I caught a glimpse of her, she would retreat speedily back into her cottage like a rabbit down its hole. I did manage to catch the postman on the odd occasion when he delivered letters, to have a chat. I often wondered to myself, after the girls left to go back to New Zealand, that if it hadn't been for 'Posty', how would anyone have known I was still alive?

I was sad to see the New Zealand girls leave, for they had become good and loyal friends to me. My solitary days, slowly passing, were indeed grim. I barely slept for the creaking of shrinking wood and the gurgling of the water in the pipes. Time dragged and I longed for Euan to return at the weekend so that I could sleep peacefully again, safely wrapped in his arms. The house also demanded much of me: fires to kindle, wood to replenish, and, most of all, I was in charge of this historical mansion, caretaker and mistress in one.

# 3

# *The Old and the New*

EUAN phoned me every evening, and on one particular night, he told me that when he returned he would be bringing a young girl to stay and work in Glentruim. The girl was a patient of a colleague of his and had been brought up in a convent. She was an orphan and had been troubled with many problems over the years. The nuns were very kind to her, but now, at the age of nineteen, they felt that it was time that she went out into the world to start life on her own.

I welcomed the new housemaid and as I showed her to her room I could not help noticing her slanted eyes, which seemed only to look from the side, beneath long unkempt strands of auburn hair. She was plainly dressed in a white blouse over black trousers and walked with an awkward gait. All the while her lips formed a smile, yet she did not seem to smile, which was somewhat unnerving.

I left the new girl to unpack and told her that I would be back shortly to see how she was getting on. From her quarters I took the back stairs down to the door going into the kitchen, where Euan was unloading food boxes. As he handed me vast quantities of food to place in the freezer, I told him I thought that the young girl looked very strange. I also wondered whether she would settle here. It was obvious that she would require a lot of supervision to begin with, as she had never been out of the convent. Indeed, the Sister Superior had mentioned to Euan that she was a good little worker, providing she was alongside someone else.

While we were in the kitchen Euan and I discussed the plans for our furniture from our cottage outside Edinburgh, which was to be sold the very next week. We had planned to place the sitting-room furniture in the boudoir, which would at least give me one room of comfortable and familiar pieces. Also Euan intended to go to the 'sale rooms' to pick up some antiques and other useful items to spread around the place. He was always good at this; our cottage had been well furnished with antiques and things that 'could be valuable one day'!

Euan went from room to room measuring and visualizing the pieces of furniture we required and I went back up to see how the new maid was managing. I knocked on her door and, receiving no answer, eventually entered to find her sitting on her bed, coat still on and suitcase untouched.

I remember offering to assist her with the unpacking. I got no reaction at all and so, without waiting for a reply, I opened her suitcase and began to place her neatly folded clothes into drawers. Work of the nuns, I had thought, everything so crisp and clean, all so meticulously ironed.

After the unpacking was completed, I coaxed our new protégé into going down to the kitchen for something to eat and assured her that after supper she could go back and settle in her room for the night. She made no eye contact and must have felt very out of place and bewildered. There were not many words exchanged with her that evening; it was hard to get more than a 'yes' or a 'no' and, if at all, it was only in the form of a nod or a shake of the head. She retired early. Tomorrow would be more promising, I hoped.

The next day was not much better for our new employee. By 9.30 that morning there was no sign of her and I found her in her bed, still dressed in her day clothes. This behaviour instigated the first of many a little 'talking-to', as difficult for me, I suspect, as for her! I felt that she might be more than I had bargained for. Over the following days, however, I began to get a response for

18

she could work hard when she wanted to, but as the nuns had said, supervision was essential. If I left her for any length of time at all she would come to a standstill and await instructions. My pregnancy made me slow and I found this whole business quite exhausting.

When the deal for our cottage had been concluded, our furniture was delivered to Glentruim, although furniture from a cottage hardly filled a mansion house. Nevertheless, little as it was, it was very welcome. It began to feel truly like home. The large drawing room was unfortunately still sparse, with only the Broadwood grand piano from my parents' home, and a large display cabinet. Also the bare floorboards in this room caused it to have a distinctive echo of emptiness. On the other hand, the boudoir looked most inviting with our old sitting-room furniture. This was then the room I tended to use in the evenings, settling down in front of the neat blue-tiled fireplace with its black marble mantlepiece. A glass door led into the conservatory, where honeysuckle had crept through a gap in one of the windows and would be the source of soft fragrances in the spring. From the far side of the conservatory one could see visitors approaching up the avenue, and from the left there was that captivating view down across the lawns to the valley below, which stretched far over towards the Cairngorms.

Not long after we had arrived at Glentruim, Euan found a room full of un-hung family portraits and paintings. This room was in the tower and both windows had, curiously, been boarded up. We presumed that Aunt Katie had used this as a darkroom. She had been a keen photographer, and in the basement there were numerous porcelain developing-dishes. The views from the two windows in this room were stunning. One looked up over the torr across to Craig Dhu and the other looked down the Spey Valley. Although badly in need of decoration, this room was charming. The pictures were soon established in their rightful places on the walls of Glentruim, even in rooms which awaited furniture.

With so much time to spare I spent many a day exploring basement, grounds and out-houses and was rewarded by the find of some real treasures. It was odd how some of the very old pieces of furniture had been considered dated and replaced by those far less valuable. Even more strange how exquisite hand-painted tables had been covered with Fablon and confined to the dungeons. Most of these pieces had to be restored in some way or another.

It was on one of my days of exploring in the old laundry, just behind the coach house and stables, when I found one of the biggest treasures. The large old key had to be placed in the lock upside-down and turned the wrong way to gain access. Grass growing through the bottom of the door made it stiff to open, but, once in, it was like peeping into the past. The old boilers in the corner of the room could probably still be stoked and fired. Everywhere else lay farm implements which had seen better days, a selection of gardening tools and discarded broken furniture, all in disarray. Horse panniers hung from the rafters, as did bundles of string, strips of cloth and all sorts of unwanted articles. I had never seen such cobwebs, stretching from one item to the other, over ledges, down doors and across broken window-panes. There was straw scattered all over the place, on the floor and over furniture. In the corner I spotted an object, very large and totally submerged in straw. Curiosity got the better of me, and in spite of my dread of spiders, being careful where I trod, I tentatively brushed off some of the straw with an old broom. It was a store for potatoes! But what was under the potatoes, I wondered? To my delight I found the two ends of the original dining-room table, which had been placed together to make a round surface top. They were white with mildew and badly marked, but, once I had organised their return to the dining-room, I got to work on restoring them. With the aid of vinegar, Brasso, beeswax and plenty of elbow grease, I studiously laboured for weeks to return them to their former glory. We had already found the three middle pieces of this table, stored upright in a specially-constructed cupboard, hidden behind the pantry dresser. Once this table was put together again, twenty could sit very comfortably around it for dinner. The matching chairs were all over the place, in out-houses, dungeons and basement, some not in perfect condition, but adequate for use. Two matching side-tables, which we placed on either side of a wall, part of an archway, in the hall, were also found in this way, as was a tallboy, many marble wash-stands, along with their irreplaceable ornate china bowls, soap dishes, jugs and chamber pots. There was also a selection of other not very exciting but useful odds and ends dotted around in hidden places.

On Friday nights I could hardly contain my excitement, while waiting for Euan to return home, to tell him of each new find. The loneliness and fatigue seemed insignificant on days such as those, when time had been well-spent and productive.

Many a weekend would be taken up by exploring together. It was not long before the end of my pregnancy that we shared a very thrilling discovery in the ballroom. This room was situated above one of the farm steadings and could only be reached by a ladder from the outside of the building, through a loft space, since the staircase was far too unsafe to attempt. A tricky climb when so heavily pregnant! Euan went first and I could see by his face that he had spied something very special. It was his great-grandfather's horse-driven sleigh. This sleigh had come from Russia and was one of a pair, the other having belonged to Cluny Estate. Returning to the house we went to the hall to look at the painting of this very sleigh, with his great-grandfather and great-grandmother being driven across the snow by two beautiful horses. The bells shown on the horses' tack, in the painting, were placed above the picture frame. A satisfying day it had been; our history was unfolding and our home was gradually becoming more complete with the new and the old blending together.

21

It must have been great fun and also very grand, having one's own ballroom. There was certainly no grandeur left, when I looked in that day, from my precarious position on the top of the ladder. This vast room, with high ceiling and wooden floor, had nothing left apart from remnants of the once velvet-seated benches, where rest would have been taken between dances. I believe the old Glentruim Lairds used to give a prize to the person who danced the most at the Glentruim Balls and I also heard from one of the villagers that the prize was often in the form of a gold watch.

The early spring had given me more opportunity to get out for walks with the dogs, while the housemaid was left to see what she could achieve on her own with the housework. Over the months I found that she was becoming unhealthily attached to me and that it proved very difficult to have any time for myself. She would follow me everywhere and expected my full attention, just like a child. Even my sheltie was a source of jealousy.

One day, making my escape from the girl, I went out with both dogs, slowly making my way up to the family graveyard, which was reached through a path in the birch wood. The graveyard stood high on a hill and commanded incredible views across the valley and to the wide flowing River Spey below. I loved this walk, the smell of birch filling my nostrils as the dogs rushed excitedly in front of me, scattering fallen leaves beneath their paws. Half way up I had the misfortune to meet The Sparrow walking her dog too. I could feel a surge of adrenaline, my 'fight or flight' reaction, in readiness for an unfriendly encounter. The dogs once again had to be pulled off each other before damage was done. The Sparrow, predictably, scuttled back down the path to her cottage. No words answered my polite greetings. Once I got to my destination I composed myself, as I rested on one of the mounting-blocks at the side of the graveyard gates. I thought how senseless this whole situation had become. The Sparrow was my nearest neighbour and yet the most hostile person I had ever known. Could we ever be friends? Perhaps I should make the effort. I stayed for a while taking in the exhilarating country air and beautiful scenery before making my way back home with a definite plan in mind. I put a lead on each dog and, with my heart pounding, I knocked on her door. A face only appeared, peeping from behind the scarcely-opened door.

'Miss Sparrow,' I said feebly, tightening the hold on my dogs, then more bravely inquired, 'Could we not be friends? Would you like to come for afternoon tea?'

'No, I would *not*,' she shrieked, 'you are *no* Lady!' And with that the door was slammed in my face. I could barely restrain the tears from spilling down my cheeks as I humbly retraced my tracks home. Clearly I could never replace her former 'Lady' of the House, but Lady of the House I was, albeit young and new. Yes, I was very young, at the age of twenty-five, for this new position of mine. No friends, no neighbours – only a very unstable girl to keep watch over. It seemed that this teenager was to be my only source of companionship.

# 4

# *The Housemaid*

OUR first-born arrived in the spring of 1972. Before this great event I had spent many a day with the young girl in the house, helping her adjust both to her new environment and to the work she was employed to do. It was no easy exercise, having her by my side, supervising, advising and in many ways 'mothering' her. She identified with me like a newborn babe, resenting attention given to any other single living creature in this world of hers, which she apparently shared with me alone. I could see the warning signs. I had spent too much time alone with her; I had in effect brought about this uncomfortable situation. Because she behaved like a trusting child, how could I suddenly become detached, hence leaving her vulnerable and at risk, not only to herself, but to circumstance? With the baby's birth imminent, I was worried that she would not be able to cope on her own until my return from the hospital – that she would be completely confused and unhappy. We had to arrange for someone, in my absence, to come and look after our home and also this adolescent. Great friends of ours, both retired, willingly agreed. To be in such picturesque countryside and live in such a historic building was their dream.

The day before I travelled down to Edinburgh, the Patersons arrived to take over. I met them at the door and was about to show them around when we heard a shrill, long howl, which echoed throughout the house. I immediately thought of my sheltie. Excusing myself from our friends, I hurriedly went in search of Crubie. I could find him nowhere. Eventually my instinct, which I tried not to believe, was correct and it took me to the maid's room. My urgency too great to knock, I barged in. There he was.

I questioned the girl, knowing full well that she had hurt the dog. A sullen look, veering downwards, answered my question. Taking a quivering Crubie in my arms, I went back downstairs to the main hall where the Patersons stood with their bags, still waiting to be shown to their rooms. I had warned the Patersons of this girl's behaviour before they had agreed to come. They had both worked in mental hospitals and were very capable of handling difficult behaviour, so I knew that they would deal with everything admirably.

I was unprepared for the send-off when I left the next day. All of the old retainers had been primed by Euan and were at the front door, wishing me the best. This in itself was an unexpected surprise, but their farewell words sought unspoken promises. Without exception they all remarked, 'See you home with your son and heir,' and one by one they shook my hand. This was not so much a question as a statement, which will remain with me forever. Down the long avenue and down the hundred miles and more to Edinburgh those farewell words haunted me. To them it seemed most natural; to me it was a foreboding. What would happen if I gave birth to a daughter? I wondered. Would I be letting them down? It was expected of me, a boy and heir was expected! A boy – could I deliver? I trembled, just as I had on my journey up, but this was not in anticipation: this was in fear of failure. Tradition told me what was to be expected, but intuition told me events would overrule.

A girl was born, Catriona Helen Marie. A girl – how could I face them all? When I should have been peacefully content, I was filled with trepidation about my return. I knew that Euan was ecstatic; to him our babe was born, flesh and blood, perfect in every way. However, inwardly I could not help but wonder whether Euan had hoped for a boy too, like the retainers – a son and heir. Tradition often has no room for change, even in a modern world. Nothing was going to spoil the elation of this birth for me, I had thought, not even the expectations which determined a safe line of heritage.

With my return came pleasant surprises. All were there to greet me: the retainers and, more astonishing, The Sparrow. I had arrived tired and inevitably very tense, but the overwhelming welcome, so different to that bleak November day the previous year, filled me with pride. As I walked in, Euan teasingly said that the drawing-room ceiling had fallen in. I hoped that he was joking. I rushed into the drawing-room only to find everyone there with a glass in hand, ready to toast the new arrival. It was very moving: friendship, and a furnished, newly-decorated room. The crib stood empty and waiting at the side of the glowing fire. Warmth! I felt warmth both in Glentruim and in the presence of all around me. What a homecoming! I was truly home. How long this would last I did not care; to me it was all I could have wished for the time being. Mr Paterson had completely redecorated the drawing-room by himself, even to the extent of taking a small paintbrush to the intricate cornices and ceiling rose.

As everyone cooed over Catriona, I looked around, well-pleased with what I saw. There were the two Davenport desks, which we had brought up from Edinburgh, one in front of each long window and either side of the French doors. Euan had bought one Davenport at auction and the other he bought from the convent our housemaid had come from. The latter had been used for keeping money in, for the convent canteen. There were also two new, large green couches, an armchair and a new green carpet with a thick pile. An oval walnut table stood in front of the French doors and upright chairs were scattered around. On each side of the fireplace was a large white-painted firescreen on pedestals, under whose glass was the most exquisite embroidery, the work of Euan's great-grand aunts. These pieces, along with my parents' grand piano and display cabinet, made a very striking room.

For a moment my eyes fixed on Catriona in her rocking-cradle, which was a safe distance from the roaring fire. She looked lost in it but the little Moses basket, more suited to her size, was in the nursery. I remembered the day I had left by train to Edinburgh for an ante-natal appointment, and had decided to buy some kind of baby's cradle. The day had gone well until the return journey, when, as I got closer to Newtonmore, I thought that I should be able to spot Glentruim. At that very moment my heart sank. I saw a fire in the distance – a house-fire, always my dread at Glentruim, which was an isolated house. It was in fact the local rubbish-dump alight, but I only found this out later once I was safely home. It gave me quite a shock, but the worst of the journey was after I had got off the train. As I struggled with the Moses basket, the heel of my shoe broke. Losing my footing, I fell between the train and the platform, only to be saved by my bump.

The Patersons stayed for a few days, and their company was more than welcome. I settled our baby daughter into our room and began the motherly bonding so much talked about in the medical world. She was my world. How I wished that Euan could be there to share this delight. It was hard, almost like being a single mother, yet when Euan returned at the weekends, loneliness seemed far away; we were a family again. Catriona was a joy. As all mothers do, I felt that mine was a very special child, and, as she grew up, I found that she was not only adorable but also remarkable. From infancy it seemed she had inherited certain characteristics from her ancestors, which became clearer as time went by.

Not long after my return, the atmosphere between me and the young housemaid soured. Life with her became at best intolerable and at worst, I felt, dangerous. My first frightening experience was when an architect came to look at the old kitchen. The morning had started well and I supervised the girl in between caring for Catriona. I had told her that a gentleman was coming for lunch and that he was an architect who was going to give advice on refurbishing the kitchen. I briefly mentioned this as the housework was nearing an end. I intimated that she should have a break and go up to her room while I had the meeting with the architect in the kitchen. I was quite taken aback to hear that this was far from her mind. Then came her usual remarks, often blurted out when she felt insecure: 'You want me out of the way, you don't want me around, do you?'

I could see by her face that she was mortally offended; she neither had any intention of being sent to her room, nor under any circumstances was she going to be excluded from my company in preference to someone else. I began to get cross and insisted that she must indeed go to her room and that I should be left to my meeting. Her controlled expression and the threat to cut her wrists, as she delved into the knife drawer, made me go cold.

Confused and terrified, I tried to move her to the door to persuade her to go upstairs, but my efforts were fruitless. The only solution was to gather up all of the sharp knives from the kitchen and remove them, which I did. I marched out of the room and ventured towards the hall. My intention was to place them in the drawer of the large oak table in the centre of the hall. As I neared the table I could not help but notice the presence of someone standing at the door. It was the architect. Thanks to the drama in the kitchen, I had not heard the doorbell ring and he had just walked in. He tried not to stare at the armful of knives which I was cramming into the hall-table drawer, but his eyes were drawn to this spectacle.

Flustered, I quickly explained that the girl who worked for me was rather odd and that when we went into the kitchen together he should ignore her if she was misbehaving. I could see that he was impressed by the splendour of the great hall, with its stag heads, weapons and grand old portraits, but it was obvious that he was also trying not to show his nervousness.

I walked in front of him to the kitchen door and all I could do was hope for calm when we got there – fruitlessly as it turned out. When we entered, the girl was sitting in front of the old range, her face smeared with soot, and she was in the process of devouring the fluff around her slippers. As the architect took the tape-measure from his pocket and speedily measured the room, I could see him throw anxious looks in her direction. He did not stay for lunch!

Most of the rooms urgently required decorating, so I decided that I should get started on this as soon as possible. The most appropriate rooms to begin on, I thought, would be two in the west wing overlooking the bank facing the front door. This bank was a carpet of numerous varieties of daffodils each spring, and would be a delightful outlook. The larger room would be for us, with the smaller of the two, which had probably been a dressing-room in the past, for the baby.

I soon finished the nursery, which was at last clean and fresh with its furniture painted white and soft pastel walls. Festooned with cuddly toys, mobiles and a baby's essentials, it was then ready. As soon as our rooms were finished, we all moved into the west wing.

The next room targeted was formerly occupied by The Sparrow. I did not want a trace of her left in the place. Needless to say, she had avoided me since my homecoming party. This room deserved to be freshened; these walls should shed their memories of their past occupant for ever.

Because I had asked the housemaid on so many occasions to leave me undisturbed while I was decorating, she again vented her feelings of being unwanted. By this time my patience was sorely tried and I bolted into my room, locking myself in. I could hear her tormented wails getting louder as the weight of her whole body was perpetually driven against the door in order to burst it open. Then came a threat which shook me to the core. I even remember her very words: 'If you don't let me in, I will harm your baby.'

I panicked. She knew I would open up, for the nursery door was closer to her than to me behind my locked door. As I fumbled with the key and unlocked the door, I was faced by a look of madness. Precipitated by fear, I made a very stupid mistake. 'If you dare even touch my baby,' I unashamedly shouted, 'I have a gun and I will use it.' After Catriona was born Euan had given me an unloaded gun, which was kept under the bed, for our protection, mainly against intruders. Not that I would have known how to use it then, even if I had had ammunition.

I could not believe what I had just said. It only made matters worse, driving her totally out of control. I was shaking all over. I ran downstairs and she was at my heels, like a hound chasing a frightened fox, but at least this diverted her attention from the nursery door. In vain I tried to pick up the telephone in the boudoir but it was torn from my hands. I ran to the kitchen and held the door shut with my foot while attempting to reach the telephone on the sideboard. My foot could not hold the force behind it and again she was by my side, ripping the telephone from my grasp. She was incoherent and becoming more violent. I then feared for my own life as well as for Catriona's. I had to calm down and think rationally. An offer of a cup of tea was all I could think of. As I made the tea, I could feel my heart pounding, my mouth dry. I was almost breathless with fear. I risked turning my back on her, but although I could not see her, I could feel her eyes piercing my very soul. I placed the tea on the kitchen table and sat down. She took her cup and then stood with her back to the door, which she studiously guarded. After a suitable time had passed, I got up and asked her if she would excuse me if I went off to bed. I thought that I would never reach the boudoir at my deliberately slow pace, which I had hoped would not arouse suspicion. Once there I shut the door and quickly telephoned the doctor. Just as I had finished dialling she burst into the room. Her frenzy exceeded all, and I experienced her full strength as she terminated my call and sent me reeling across the room. I desperately searched for pacifying words, but none seemed to suit. In any case, she was not listening to anyone but herself as she rambled on incoherently. I soon noticed a beam of light momentarily shining through the conservatory door from a fast-approaching car. The doctor was quickly on the scene, having suspected that the abruptly halted call had been from me.

I tried to send this sad girl back to Edinburgh the next day, but her behaviour was outrageous. Twice she tried to get out of our newly acquired Land Rover on the way to the railway station, and then when I finally got her there she ripped off her clothes in front of all the bystanders on the platform. I had to take her home again.

Euan came home that night and I was thankful to have him there to deal with the problem at hand. The following day, however, Euan had difficulty in getting the girl into his car and had to ask the police to assist. She took off as soon as she saw the police car, but the police were in fast pursuit of her, up the bank and into the bushes. Then they too felt her force. She hit out at one and the fierce blow to the officer's face resulted in an excellent rugby tackle, which brought her down. Helmet askew, and together with the aid of the other policeman, he forced her into their car.

Doctor Orchard, the police surgeon, known fondly by the locals as 'Boysie', was waiting at the police station and was asked if he required assistance, but declined. 'Not with a young girl,' he was saying as he entered the cell. Ultimately the police were indeed required, for as soon as the doctor walked in, she

31

wrenched the telephone apparatus from the wall and hurled it across the room, striking poor old 'Boysie' on the chest!

That was her final downfall. She was collected the next day from her cell by two nuns from the convent and taken back to Edinburgh. It was not the last I saw or heard of her. Twice she ran away from the convent and landed on our doorstep. In addition, for many years afterwards, she would telephone in the middle of the night, not always to speak, but to listen to my voice.

# 5

# *The Macpherson Line*

SHORTLY before Euan and I married we discussed our age gap, which had not worried either of us. Euan had told me that he would not be the first in the Glentruim family to marry someone much younger than himself since Lachlan Macpherson of Ralia, who was born in 1723, on reaching the age of fifty-three, had married a sixteen-year-old girl. This marriage was referred to in *Church and Social Life* by Alex. Macpherson: 'Of this Lachlan it is said that on one occasion, when paying a casual visit to his neighbours, the Macphersons of Banchor, a child was lying in its cradle.' This narrative then tells of the child's mother having to attend to some household duties, but before leaving she requested, 'Rock the cradle for me, Lachlan, the little girlie may yet be your wife,' to which he replied, 'I'll certainly rock the cradle for you, but I fear I'm already too old – if I ever get married at all – to wait so long for a wife.' It was this same infant, Grace, who became Lachlan's spouse, having a considerably larger age-difference than that of Euan and me, theirs being thirty-seven years as opposed to our twenty!

Lachlan had been a JP and Deputy-Lieutenant for Inverness-shire and lived a long life, dying at the age of ninety, leaving his wife Grace with eleven children. Duncan, one of his sons, became a major in the Black Watch and James, Lachlan's youngest son, did not marry but distinguished himself through his feats of supreme daring at the storming of Badajos when, during the Peninsular War, he served under Wellington. We still have an etching on the wall describing the capture of Badajos, which relates the victory in the battle. It also tells us how James, although wounded, ascended a scaling ladder, tore down the French colour and, for lack of a substitute, hoisted his red jacket. He was presented with a medallion of rubies and pearls, set in gold, to commemorate his supreme daring and gallantry. I treasure this lovely piece of jewellery, which I wear around my neck on very special occasions! A print of those taking part in the battle of Badajos hangs in the alcove of the smoking-room at Glentruim. There is also an added interest to this picture: a tubular metal cylinder which houses a rolled-up scroll of the print, incorporating the names of every person involved in the battle.

Ewan, Lachlan's eldest son, who was born in 1782, became a major in the 42nd Madras Infantry and it was he who purchased the ruin of Glentruim from the duke of Gordon, then built the mansion that stands there today. Ewan was the first Macpherson of Glentruim, thus making his father the last Macpherson of Ralia, an estate which lies between Glentruim and Newtonmore. When Ewan died he was succeeded by Robert, who had no children, so Glentruim subsequently fell into the hands of Lachlan, Robert's younger brother, and the third to inherit the Glentruim title. He too was a military man and went to the Crimea; having served in the battles of Alma, Inkerman and Sebastopol, he received many awards for his bravery.

When looking through pieces in our own museum at Glentruim, a quarter-rial (coin) was found in a Shako, a tall quilted army dress-hat with a front visor (1862 design), which had belonged to the aforementioned Lachlan. The rial had been tucked into the hatband and inside, 'Captain Lachlan Macpherson, Captain 30th a Foot, circa 1863', had been clearly marked in ink. Perhaps the rial had been hidden there by

Lachlan, as a keepsake! Lachlan later reached the rank of colonel.

Colonel Lachlan of Glentruim had four sons and two daughters, one of the sons being my husband's father, Lachlan Oliver Norman. Euan used to tell me a wonderful tale about Lachlan's four sons, which he later retold for inclusion in a collection of Scottish family history memoirs published by the Canongate Press in 1986. The book, the result of a literary competition, was entitled *Winning Tales*, with the first prize given for Euan's contribution. He was presented with a specially commissioned painting of Glentruim House by a Scottish artist, Hugh Buchanan.

In this story Euan describes a troublesome day upon which his grandparents' four sons went missing. During the afternoon the governess had interrupted Lachlan from his quiet, thoughtful moments in the library, to ask the whereabouts of his sons. They should have been back at four o'clock, to spend two hours in the classroom. Lachlan had not seen his boys and became angered by their disobedience. As Euan used to tell me, his grandfather had been an orderly man who disliked unregulated changes of any existing arrangements. Time passed and still there was no sign of his sons. Filled with anger, he went into the smoking-room cupboard to fetch a tawse – a leather punishment strap – and laid it on his green leather-topped desk, to await his children's return.

Eventually the dark of the evening fell; the whole family was in disarray and Lady Glentruim became tearful. The Laird now struggled with emotions of both fear and anger. He asked for the bells at the coach house to be rung. The workers on the estate each had their own code of rings, one for the keeper, two for the coachman and so on. All men were summoned to Glentruim. Now Lachlan's anger had turned to unease and then to dread of what might be found as he ordered a search party for his sons.

There had been a thick fall of snow and the wind had begun to pick up, causing drifting. The keeper, weary from his day on the hill, was filled with foreboding; he felt that in such bad weather the searchers were doomed to failure. With torch in hand, he retraced his tracks of the morning but, thinking how difficult it was to find a fox or a deer in the dense undergrowth, he wondered what chance he would have at that time of night, in such conditions, of finding the boys.

Lachlan's mind began to run wild, for there were many dangers on the land and many possibilities. His sons could have walked up over the hills, sunk deep into a gulley of snow, unable to find their way home, or they might have fallen off a steep cliff-face up the torr. He could not settle: he had to join in the search. He made his way through the dark pinewoods of Nessan Tulloch, with his lamp, through to the far end of the woods where there was a path leading to the Falls of Truim. He knew that the river was swollen by the melting snow which slid down from Drumochter, and was well aware how turbulent the current could be. He imagined one of the boys losing his foot-hold and falling into a deep pool and the others trying to rescue him. They all could easily have been drowned together.

The search came to an end when the weather closed in, the men exhausted. Lachlan sat thinking of the bleak prospect of dragging the rivers in the morning, while the local doctor consoled the women in the house, giving each a small dose of laudanum to assist their sleep. Lachlan shut himself in the library and looked out of the window into the darkness of this horrible night, with tears rolling down his cheeks. He could not bear to look at the leather tawse on the desk, which he had placed there in his fit of anger earlier in the day.

Grief-stricken and limp with tiredness, he sat in the armchair by the fire and sipped his whisky from a crystal glass. He watched the flames leap high in the grate and thought of each son in turn. They were so different in character and he loved them all, in the way that a father does. He even forgave his strong-willed Evan, his eldest and rebellious son, whom he thought would have been the leader in any mischief that night. A fleeting glimpse was taken of the tawse and heavier tears followed.

The whisky glass was empty and Lachlan went over to the decanter to replenish it. The decanter too was empty, so he lit a candle and walked down the stone stairs, under the main staircase in the house, to the wine cellars in the basement. The inner cellar, which was barrel-vaulted, its floor made of cobblestones, contained not only wine but also a forty-five gallon cask of whisky. This vast vat was mounted on a wooden trestle, surrounded by wine-racks on the wall. Although the floor itself was uneven, there was something else that made Lachlan stumble. Raising his candle aloft, he found his sons lying on the floor below the whisky cask, all four in a drunken stupor!

With not a trace of anger left, only joy, Lachlan ran upstairs shouting to all who could hear him, that his sons were alive and well. Stone hot-water bottles were filled and the boys were carried up to their beds. Glentruim and his lady were at last able to go to their own bed in peace without dreading the morning. There was only one more thing that the Laird had to do before he retired for the night. He took the leather tawse from his desk and returned to the wine cellar. There he hung this instrument of retribution on a hook at the far end, beyond the whisky cask, where it was to remain forever!

The Glentruim title should have been passed to Colonel Lachlan's eldest son Evan Gordon, but because father and son fell out, proceedings were undertaken through the Lord Lyon to disinherit Evan. Thus Duncan James, the second son, inherited Glentruim. Duncan, another gallant member of the family, served in the South African War with the Scottish Imperial Yeomanry and also in the Great War of 1914–18. This brings our history up to the late 1960s when my husband, Euan, became heir to Glentruim through his Aunt Katie, who had in turn succeeded her husband, Duncan, but was left childless. Indeed Euan himself followed his military ancestors in serving his country during the Second World War, initially in the Royal Air Force, although he was later transferred to the army, which required more soldiers.

Euan's father, Lachlan, eventually married Dorothy Birch-Jones, the daughter of a clergyman. However, as Lachlan had briefly had a previous wife, and because the stern moral strictures of some of the clergy in those days permitted no divorce, Dorothy was immediately disowned by her family. These were the 'gold rush' years and Lachlan, a mining engineer, took his wife over to Canada, where he panned for gold. Both Euan and his sister, Marie, were born in Alberta, but the family returned to England when Lachlan discovered that he had cancer. Desperate for money, Dorothy accepted a job as a teacher at Shrewsbury High School, but unfortunately Euan's father died during this period in Shropshire.

Dorothy applied for a teaching post in New Zealand and was soon to sail there with her children. Regrettably, the headmistress disapproved of Dorothy arriving with her family in tow. Because it was a girls' school Marie was allowed to stay but Euan, at the age of four, was sent away to a boys' boarding school.

In 1936, the family returned to England because Dorothy had found a lump in her breast and suspected cancer. With the anxiety of her imminent death, she placed Marie in a boarding school and Euan was 'given away'. Dorothy had signed Euan over to a couple in Cheltenham, who could not have children of their own, the deal being that they would keep Euan as their son, in exchange for paying for his education at Cheltenham College. This bizarre arrangement, made in good faith, later turned out to have been superfluous, for Euan's mother discovered that she did not have cancer after all. Unfortunately, it was by then impossible to retract the agreement between herself and the couple. During this sad time, Dorothy was allowed to live with her mother in the Lake District, where she then embarked on a teaching post at Kendal High School.

Euan was very unhappy with his guardian and his wife, who did not treat him well. He was kept in an attic, with only a candle for light and was harshly punished for not being able to show the expected love of a dutiful son. Because Euan's mother could never have afforded the tuition fees, there was no choice for Euan during the years of his education at Cheltenham but to stay.

Euan's days with his guardian were soon to come to an end when he was caught kissing a girl behind the bicycle shed at the college! Although this in itself was not such a crime, it was the fact that she was the baker's daughter and not an educated girl that precipitated Euan's expulsion. He was only sixteen, but fortunately had already achieved the necessary qualifications to enter Edinburgh University. He immediately ran away to Edinburgh, but not before confronting his guardian. He reminded him of the torment and cruelty that he had had to endure from him, adding that he never wanted to see him again in his life. Apparently there was even a fist thrust at his tormentor, knocking him to the ground, a small act of vengeance which gave Euan great satisfaction.

Not long after Euan had started at Edinburgh University, conscription took him to war. I remember Euan telling me of his time at army camp and how they all fought for the beds nearest the open fire in their billet. Many of the men were ex-convicts, who were horribly dangerous. The 'college' boys, whom they saw as their superiors, always had the last say, but sometimes the upper hand was only gained by engaging in fist-to-fist confrontations.

It must have been a trying time for Euan, particularly because he suffered rheumatic heart disease while at camp. He was subsequently demobbed and then hospitalised for over a year. When he was eventually discharged, the doctors told him that if he looked after himself, resting as much as possible and walking upstairs backwards, then he might live for two years! For Euan this was a dim prospect, so he decided to live his predicted short span to the full, with little regard for his health or safety. He went skiing, sailing, carried out reckless rock-climbs and did everything that he had always longed to do, in other words all the activities that he should not have engaged in, according to the doctors. He survived those two years very well indeed, thereafter carrying on with his life as any other normal, healthy person.

Euan always knew that he would inherit Glentruim: the place meant everything to him and he most certainly loved it. It felt right that he should be there, in his ancestral home, with all its history, and I too was soon ensnared in this web of the past. We were soon, however, to discover that our future held not only joy but also a great deal of anguish.

# 6

# *The Northern Folk*

ON happy days, but particularly on sad days, I would walk to the torr and sit in my favourite place, on the mounting block outside the family graveyard. How tranquil it was there, by the spirits of Macphersons, with what I believed to be the most dramatic views in Badenoch. It was on one of these 'sad' days, feeling desperately alone and sorry for myself, that I walked up there with dogs and pram. How one's mind drifts when loneliness invades it. Devouring the expanse of Scottish countryside, tears welled up in my eyes, blurring my vision, before trickling down my cheeks, only to be halted by the curve of my lips. Tasting the salt, I wiped away the tears, and as clearer eyes scanned the 'Macpherson Country', I dwelled on parts of history which were very much talked of then and still are today amongst the Macpherson strongholds.

Reminders of those days, well noted in our history books, were marked all around me. Euan so often talked about 'Cluny's Whiskers', known to some clan members as 'Cluny's Toothbrush', which were in view at the far end of the valley in the form of trees on the crest of the hill above Catlodge. These trees were planted there some time between 1820 and 1830 to commemorate the departure to India of Old Cluny's youngest brother, Archibald Fraser Macpherson. There was a protective wall around the site, which represented a major effort by a large number of people back at that time. However, many a gale had

41

brought down trees over the years and Cluny's Whiskers were becoming sparse. The tombstones and large granite memorials to past Glentruims, descendents from the youngest brother of Cluny, were right behind me in the graveyard as I sat with my thoughts.

Then there were the numerous hiding places used by Ewan Macpherson of Cluny, known as 'Cluny of the Forty-five'. He was a notable leader in the Loyalist army and, after Culloden, was accorded the distinction of being valued at a thousand guineas, dead or alive. Although he was near to capture on several occasions, no one betrayed him. One of the houses, named Dalchully, in which Old Cluny hid was to be found much further down the valley beyond Cluny's Whiskers. It was a memorable event when Sir Hector Munro, from the opposition, went in search of Old Cluny and, having arrived at Dalchully, on horseback, had the house surrounded by his cavalry. Sir Hector ordered everyone to come out, and Cluny, with no time to reach his secret room, put on one of his servants' coats and offered to hold Sir Hector's horse. Old Cluny, mistaken as a servant, was asked if he had seen 'Cluny', to which he replied, 'No, I have not, and if I had seen him, I would not tell you.' Sir Hector replied, 'I don't believe you would, you're a fine fellow, and here's a shilling for you.' An inspiring tale, and to commemorate that day a large silver model was made of the Highlander holding the horse, with the figure of Sir Hector in the saddle handing Cluny the shilling piece. This great épergne was the work of Clark Stanton, and was esteemed as one of the finest examples of a silversmith's craft anywhere in Europe. It was presented to Old Cluny at his golden wedding in 1782 by his clansmen and now takes pride of place in the Clan Museum at Newtonmore.

Looking across to the other side of the Spey from where I sat was the south side of Craig Dhu, translated as 'black rock' ('Craig Dhu' was in fact used as the war cry of the Macphersons).

On this rockface, directly opposite a small loch called Lochain Ovie (situated on the bank of the Spey), was one of the caves where Cluny used to hide. After the battle of Culloden in 1746, Ewan, who was the eighteenth chief, spent many nights over the following nine years in this small, cramped cave. Clansmen from all over the world continue to make the precarious trek up to that cave during the annual Macpherson Clan Gathering.

Breakachy, meaning 'the speckled field', is the last farm in Glentruim Estate, off the back road, and many years ago used to belong to people called the MacNivens. It is said that they had a disagreement with the Macphersons of Cluny, cut out the tongue from one of the Macphersons' bulls, and also sheared the petticoats belonging to Cluny's daughter! Following this ridicule the Macphersons of Cluny massacred the MacNivens at Breakachy. It was then that Breakachy came into the hands of the Macphersons. I believe that the three daughters of this family made clothes for Bonnie Prince Charlie!

In much later years, the Shepherd's Cottage at Breakachy was found to have two rooms which had been boarded up below the sitting-room. Being so large it was suspected that they had contained an illicit still for whisky. It was also presumed that whisky would have been taken from here to Cluny Macpherson when he was in hiding on the hill. Also, around the corner, on the way up to Dalwhinnie, there is a little cottage that used to be called the 'Splash'. This was a beer house for regular travellers and is well remembered by the older people of the area. There is now even a magazine, called *The Laggan Splash,* produced locally, which depicts stories of the past along with local news and attractions.

The Laggan to Newtonmore road lies between Craig Dhu itself and Craig Dhu House, a handsome granite mansion. Penny Weir, wife of the Hon. Douglas Weir, who then lived at Craig Dhu, turned out to be one of my best friends in the area, and she was the first person to invite me to tea to meet some of the local folk. The day I got the invitation, by telephone, was the same day on which I had received a letter from one of my harp-playing friends. I had been a member of a clarsach group in Edinburgh and took great pleasure in playing this instrument. In the letter my friend gave me Penny's name and telephone number so that I could contact her. It transpired they had both been friends for many years. I still had the letter in my hand that day when the telephone rang and I gladly accepted the invitation, carefully noting instructions as to how to get to the house.

After taking Penny's call, I placed the heavy black receiver in its cradle and started to think back to the first time that I had heard of the clarsach. I had always wanted to play the harp but had never sought out information about it. One autumn evening back in 1969 I had been ill in bed, and Euan had attended a pre-arranged Gaelic Society function on his own, in the Surgeons Hall in Edinburgh. At this dinner, a beautiful young girl with long flowing hair, wearing a dark green velvet dress, sat and sang to the dinner guests accompanying herself on the clarsach. Euan was very much taken both with the girl and with the lovely music. When he came home that night he could speak of nothing else. Alison Kinnaird was the musician, and it was then that I decided to take up the clarsach. Life being full of coincidences, when I talked about the clarsach to my nurse tutor, Mary Lochead, once back at work, I learnt that not only did she play this instrument, but that she could put me in touch with a tutor. I hired a clarsach until Christmas that year, when Euan gave me my very own. By the shape of the curtains in the sitting-room in our little cottage, on Christmas Eve, I had guessed what they were hiding – it could only have been a clarsach!

Craig Dhu House was only a stone's-throw away as the crow flies, but to drive there I had to go into the nearest village and around the other side of the Spey. I found the drive, as fore-warned, on a bad corner. When I drove up to the house and past the front door I remembered feeling a sinking sensation in my stomach. I was nervous at the sight of four parked cars. I should have guessed that I would not be the only guest. Company at last, I thought, but I had mixed feelings. It had been a long time since I had been in the company of adults exchanging light conversation, and afternoon tea and coffee mornings had never been my forte. I never had enjoyed gossip or trivia, but then, perhaps I had always been too busy back in my nursing days.

The house, like its owner, was full of colour. There were bright pictures on the walls, a mixture of modern and antique furniture, and a vast open fire in the sitting-area, which must have once been a large hallway. There were three ladies engrossed in conversation by the fire and they were all talking at once with raised voices. One had a particularly loud voice and another had a rounded English accent. All were far too involved to notice my arrival, until I was introduced by our hostess. I did not absorb their names at first, feeling too out of place, a stranger in their midst. There were children of various sizes and ages briefly running in and out. Who belonged to whom was too early for me to tell. I duly listened for some time, nodding or shaking my head appropriately, while hearing about the 'bags' at the last shoot, the new children's clothes-catalogues, the latest designer knit-wear, favourite recipes, dinner-parties, local gossip and the like. Afternoon tea parties were not much different for me then than they had been before: small talk was definitely not my scene.

One young woman, about my age I thought, had a round face with bright rosy cheeks, straight shoulder-length auburn hair and a fly-away fringe. It was Sally Haywood, who I imagined to be a figure of the outdoors, hardy and 'horsey', and was sporting the latest design in knitwear, no doubt, covered in rabbits! She was a very friendly and open character, who had not long had her first baby. An invitation to tea was freely offered. I wondered whether she was just being polite and if indeed she would follow up her invitation. Many an invitation at a gathering such as this falls by the wayside, no matter how well intended.

I hardly spoke to the other two, perhaps in their thirties, both well-dressed, one in fine lady's 'plus-two's', the other in tartan trousers, very much the Barbour and green welly types. The smaller of the two was from London; an attractive lady with fine features, she was dramatically drawing on her cigarette through a long jet-black holder and blowing out through the side of her mouth as she threw her head up in laughter. The taller seemed to be a genuine, kind person, with a magnificent figure, wearing a stunning wide black belt around her narrow waist. But she had a fixed, troubled look on her brow, as if she had the burdens of the world on her shoulders.

After tea we all thanked our hostess, put on our coats and headed for home. Back in the car, I acclimatised quickly to the fall in temperature and thought of the cold that awaited me at home, with no lit fire to go back to. As I unlocked the front door, all was dark, with no one to greet me. A fire had to be lit immediately to bring cheer into the evening. When I later sat by the boudoir fire and thought about my afternoon and those there, who had full lives and established friendships, I felt even more alone.

It was not long, barely a week, before Sally invited me to her home for tea. She lived then with her husband, Mike, at Netherwood, a house up the Glen Road in Newtonmore, our nearest village. The following year they moved into one of their larger farm houses in Glenbanchor. They too had a large estate which not only included farms, but also shooting and fishing. I was keen to see how they managed their business, and if perhaps I could get some ideas to build up our depleted income.

I had gathered that Sally and Mike had not been married very long. They had met when Sally was organising pony-trekking in the area for a person called Cameron Ormiston. Cameron was one of the pioneers of pony-trekking in the Highlands, which turned out to be a highly successful tourist attraction. Sally was a good homemaker, her house very comfortable and the larders

46

complete with the previous year's jams and home-produce. But, what struck me most in her house was her tapestry work. She had made so many cushions and stool-covers, with animals, flowers and picturesque scenes, I presumed that she must have had much spare time in the quieter months of the year.

It was with Sally that I met Suzie Curtis, a lovely, caring person, with deep brown eyes and curly black hair. I took to Suzie immediately, and the feeling must have been mutual because she offered to come and help me, when she could manage, whether with the new baby or even just to come for a chat. So Suzie and I became great friends over the years and she often came to see me when she was on holiday from teaching, in a preparatory school in the South. Her father, Peter, who was not much older than Euan, became a very good friend of his. He was a brigadier and of the old school, much like Euan. There were not many such old-fashioned gentlemen as Peter and Euan in this new age that we lived in: perfect manners, gracious, with so much tradition and history in their past.

The landowners in Badenoch were very much ruled by the shooting seasons, which entailed hard work and entertaining paying guests until the off-seasons came around. Then it was the time to catch up with the neighbouring estate-owners and finish the seasonal contents of the deep-freeze at private dinner-parties. Salmon, trout, venison and all game soon became common produce, not a luxury, as it was in the cities.

We slowly got to know the party circuit, and dinner invitations came in, but only when Euan was around. It was possible to continue a conversation from one party to the next, since the same people were sure to be there.

Euan was always such a good conversationalist and could talk about anything in great depth. Being a natural writer and poet, he hated the misuse of the English language and he spoke most eloquently. I was always extremely proud of him, but as far as experience and language went, I lagged miserably behind. How glad I was to have him by my side to support me when I floundered!

The local shopkeepers were very courteous and kind to me. I had kept on all of the accounts with the butcher, the dairy, the grocer and others. The grocer's shop belonged to and was run by the two MacRae brothers, and they really gave one preferential treatment. I loved the way, when you went into their shop, that they scampered around, fetching the produce from the shelves to put on the counter for you, and then finally into a box. If they were not busy then they even ran out to the car and placed the box in the car for you. At the garage your car would be filled with petrol, a luxury these days, and at the end of the month you received a bill, as you did from all tradesmen. It was a friendly village, but I knew it might take years before I was accepted. No problem for Euan: he was Glentruim after all. It was also an important factor to the locals that as we resided permanently at Glentruim and were not 'absentee landlords', they could be sure of our custom.

Life was turning out to be so very different for me now, with much to learn about both the environment and the inhabitants. I felt that I had stepped into a story-book and was living someone else's life, but when, I wondered, would it be mine?

I had sat on the torr long enough; hours had passed and both dogs' and baby's timetables were veering towards their lunch-hour. I could have sat there for much longer, reminiscing, but it was a morning well-spent, since by then I felt much better. I had counted my blessings and was ready to go forward. Glentruim was now my life, both man and heritage.

# 7

# *The Marching Army*

AS I tidied our bedroom in the west wing, thinking how chilly it was, I remembered the day I had decided to decorate it, with a view to moving in. I had felt that it would be sad to leave the bedroom at the front of the building; this new room was not so grand, smelled musty and was extremely cold. Also, it was a pity to leave behind the old half-tester bed, which must have been in the family for hundreds of years. I had found the bed in a corner of the stables, not long after I found the dining-room table in the old laundry. It was in pieces, and the drapes had been eaten away by moths. We had restored it after Catriona was born and had placed it in our bedroom. I shall never forget that day. Suzie Curtis had come to stay for a few days, and we watched Euan, along with one of the estate workers, piece together this amazing work of art. At the top of the backdrop stretched the bed-head, made of rosewood, as was the foot. The scarlet canopy hung behind and complemented long scarlet curtains at each side, which could be drawn halfway down the bed to act as a draught-excluder. This bed matched the dressing table and wardrobe, which had already been in the room. The only other piece of furniture in there was one of the old painted French tables, covered on top by the inevitable Fablon. When the bed had eventually been erected, held together with foot-long bolts, the head looked dangerously precarious, leaning about forty-five degrees over the rest. I could see by Suzie's expression that her thoughts were the same as mine.

We were both visualizing where it would strike if it fell, so we moved the baby's crib some distance away from the bed. In time it was put right, but until then it gave me just one more source of worry at night when Euan was away from home.

I recalled carefully examining our future bedroom and wondering whether I could ever feel comfortable in it. There was a certain intangible inhibition which had kept me from opening the door those few months since our arrival, let alone entering. What had given the room such a chill that made one feel so unwelcome? I wondered whether it was because it had been neglected, with no carpet, faded curtains and damp patches on the walls, or merely because it had been left empty.

A massive old mahogany companion occupied one whole side of this large room. Possibly it could be dismantled, since it would never have fitted through a door or window. There were wardrobes at each end of this companion, which opened by pulling on their carved pillars. In the middle there were three large drawers and above them a compartment with sliding doors and a secret little cupboard inside. Before the room was refurbished there was only this piece of furniture and a square gilt-framed mirror over the mantlepiece to tell its secrets, the remaining furniture having deserted its roommates.

I recalled wandering around, making plans for restoring the room, listening to my footsteps on the bare floorboards, every tiny sound exaggerated by the gloomy emptiness. I had almost felt resentment accompanying the shudder down my back that day; however, it was appropriate to move into this room, since it was closest to the nursery and in earshot of Catriona. I had measured the window for new curtains and estimated the amount of wallpaper and paint required. Then, picturing in my mind the furniture, the fabrics and all of the colours I would introduce, I was eager to begin.

After tidying up, I had inspected the nursery next door. Yes, it was perfect for an infant. The almost clinical look of cotton-wool, nappies and piles of white towels was nicely contrasted by the pretty pink flowery curtains and the pale rose-coloured wallpaper. On the left sat a small, white-painted chest-of-drawers and a low nursing chair, with a merry chintz cushion firmly secured with ribbons around the back. The crib stood in the corner, behind the door, its yards of white lace quite capable of sheltering the babe from the incorrigible draughts. Along the opposite wall sat an old ottoman, which was covered in a fabric depicting brightly-coloured birds. This was a most useful piece of furniture, with ample room for clothes inside and a large seat on top for changing nappies. It was a cosy little room, but the door had to be closed smartly on entering or leaving to avoid the warmth being grabbed by the poorly-heated corridors. Walking over to the window I had looked out at the copper beech and the ancient wellingtonia, which surged upwards, stirring gently in the wind, straight and tall, and looking indestructible against any winter storm. Below them was a mass of rhododendrons, which gave such abundance of colour each year, following the splash of golden yellow daffodils, which bloomed earlier, as if in a rush to get their show in first.

Back in our room again, I remembered thinking how dark and depressing the room was when I was decorating. When the stubborn paper gradually peeled away from the walls, it had looked even more sombre and forlorn. With the layers came years of dust, causing a very unpleasant atmosphere and, indeed, Ian Richardson, our local doctor, used to inform me that amongst the dust grew unhealthy spores in the walls. Even the wide-open windows, allowing the warmth of the summer air and the fragrances of the season to enter, did not lift the chill or the mustiness of this bleak room. Again I had to reassure myself that once it was fresh with paint and wallpaper it would feel more inviting.

For almost 120 years the wallpaper had survived the wear and tear of time, as confirmed by the signature of the painter on the bare walls. Not far from his signature was another, large and scrawling, quite obviously that of a child. Because of the dates, I had thought that it could have been one of Euan's great grand-aunts, at the age of five. Perhaps, having been allowed to watch the painter, she had wished to follow suit. I found it irresistible to do likewise, for history's sake, and had added my name and the date to the two already there. When I added my name I thought about those who had signed before me and wondered what would have been said then if the 'Lady of the House' had been the decorator. It would have been unheard of. Glentruim seemed to be full of such reminders of the past, this being just one of many. As caretaker of these precious memories, I knew how important it was to treasure them all.

Our new bedroom was certainly freshened up and a faint smell of paint lingered on. There were tiny roses in neat rows on the new wallpaper, and the traditional stained floor-surrounds shone brightly around a thick, deep-pink carpet. On the right remained the great mahogany companion, now facing long velvet curtains, of a soft pink which toned with the cover on the bed and its canopy. Two matching antique dressing-tables stood either side of the window and there was still room for a free-standing mirror (which my mother had bought at Perth Sales for £3), two easy chairs, bedside commode-tables with marble tops, and a deep-red chaise longue at the foot of the bed. The gilt-framed mirror also remained in the room above the fireplace, which had a fresh coat of black-lead. Standing back and noting the improvements, I was satisfied that the room now looked cared-for. However, there still remained a chill despite the added luxury of a Dimplex radiator.

I always did have acute hearing, but in this room I found it almost unbearable. At night there were the normal noises of an old building, but to me they were unduly sharp. I was also conscious of other sounds which I had never heard before, such as the electricity pylons humming half a mile away, cars on distant roads and even the tread of animals in the woods. The tick of watches and clocks seemed to drum in my ears, echoing back at me persistently as soon as my head touched the pillow. All sounds seemed to be trapped in this old room, yet it was not as old as the main building, having been added at a later date.

It was then May, but it was cold and there was frost on the ground. Euan was home for the weekend, but unfortunately he had a very bad toothache. On that particular night we spent a while together by the fire, then decided to retire for the night in the hope that his pain would be gone by the morning. After a few drams and a sleeping-tablet, he managed to keep the toothache at bay and achieved sleep. I popped in to see Catriona before going to bed and then, being very tired, I immediately dropped into a sound sleep.

It must have been well after midnight that I was woken by turmoil outside. For a moment or two I lay there, trying to determine whether I was totally awake and if there was actually something to be heard. Once convinced of my initial sensation, I slowly got up, listening, listening all the time. While doing so, I searched the room for any glimmer of light, but it was extremely dark, with not even a shadow to fix my eye on. Sitting on the edge of the bed I felt for my slippers with my feet and then leaned over to get my dressing-gown from the chair beyond my bedside table. Louder and louder the sounds became until they seemed almost in the room. I tried to wake Euan, shaking him furiously, but there was no response. It was unquestionably the sound of marching and it was coming even closer. Rushing to the window, I opened the curtains to detect where the noise was coming from, but, straining my eyes in order to see what my ears were telling me, I saw nothing. Determined to seek out these intruders, I hastily crossed the room, dodging furniture as I went, and reached the bedroom door. The narrow corridor from our bedroom led me to the landing at the top of the front staircase, and down those numerous steps I went in pursuit of an answer. The journey to the foot of the staircase appeared to take longer than usual and the breadth of each step made me feel uncomfortably alone and vulnerable. I came out in a cold sweat as I made my way across the front hall, towards the large windows on either side of the inner front doors. I opened the heavy braided curtains and then lifted the metal levers to open the well-used shutters. There was not a sound as I opened the shutters, only the tick of the grandfather clock in the hall, nor was there any explanation for me as I searched in vain into the blackness of the night. All was silent, all asleep. It was only I who was stirring. I could not help wondering if I had been dreaming after all. Wearily I went back upstairs, my heart still racing from the rush and excitement. Retracing my tracks, I soon reached our bedroom door and all was peaceful. Quietly I turned the door handle, so as not to waken anyone, and began to enter our room, but before my hand left the handle I was aware of disquiet. I walked straight into a shattering noise. I desperately stared all around, hoping to identify the source of the sounds and to conquer my fear. The room almost shook with the disturbance. I heard unruly thundering of feet and felt an overpowering presence of clansmen marching. I could not see them, but I sensed them all around me, brushing off me, pushing, clambering, urgent to reach their goal. I was stifled and felt crushed by the spirits of fierce warriors striding through. Rigid, I stood hugging myself tightly, willing and praying that it would all cease. Gradually I felt the room being released from this extraordinary presence, and I was exhausted by my experience. Bewildered and limp with fatigue, I climbed back into bed. All the while, Euan slept blissfully unaware. Sleep was hard to come by during the hours of night left to me as I lay there, these happenings preying on my mind. Not so much the presence of the unknown, but more the extreme discomfort to my ears and the turbulence in the room was what unnerved me that night.

As I presented Euan with his breakfast tray, having inquired about his tooth, I began to tell him what I had been through as he slept so deeply. I told him that I could not imagine how he could have slept through it all, but I did also wonder whether it was for my ears only! Euan hardly ate his breakfast; he was engrossed in thought. He sat in silence for a few moments, then he searched his memory before extracting pieces of history. I was asked to go down to the library and fetch two books, one on clan battles and the other called *Anderson's Guide to the Highlands*, published in 1850.

When I returned, Euan read aloud to me, and this is what he read from the books. The first extract was from *Anderson's Guide*, which documented the events leading up to the Battle of Invernahavon in 1386.

At Invernahavon, near the junction of the rivers Truim and Spey, a celebrated battle was fought, in the reign of James I, between the Mackintoshes and Camerons. The lands of Mackintosh, in Lochaber, were possessed by a set of Camerons who always refused to pay their rents, which were accordingly levied by force, and consisted principally of cattle. Acknowledging no right but that of occupancy, and provoked by the seizure of their herds, the Camerons at length resolved on making reprisals; and they, therefore, poured down upon Badenoch above 400-strong, headed by a Charles Magilony. The Laird of Mackintosh, thus obliged to call out his followers, soon appeared with a force sufficient for the emergency. The Davidsons of Invernahavon and the Macphersons of Cluny contended for the right hand in the line of battle; and Mackintosh, as umpire, having decided in favour of the former, the whole Clan Macpherson withdrew from the field in discontent. From the equality of numbers thus created, the conflict was sharp and bloody; many of the Mackintoshes, and almost all the

Davidsons, were killed. The Macphersons, provoked at seeing their brave kinsmen nearly overpowered, rushed in, and totally defeated the Camerons, whose leader they pursued to Glen Banchor, and overtook and slew him on a hill still called by his name, Corharlich, or Charles' hill.

Before he read the second passage, Euan looked up to tell me that because the Mackintoshes and Davidsons had suffered such great slaughter and, being totally enraged by both the Macphersons and naturally the Camerons, Mackintosh had plotted to incite the Macphersons to draw their swords against the Camerons. To achieve this, Mackintosh sent a bard with a poem to the Macphersons, claiming he had a message from the Clan Cameron, and it read:

> The traytors stood on the knoll
> While the dismayed were in jepordie
> It was not your friendship for me
> But your cowardice which restrained you.

The Macphersons were infuriated by these words, Euan said, and thus had planned their attack on the Camerons, setting off silently before midnight, during the hours of darkness, to pursue them.

Invernahavon, pronounced Invernah'an, is situated in the bottom fields to the north-east of Glentruim. Euan had told me about the battle on a previous occasion, when he found a rusty old sword in that area. My mind raced through the dates and the era when Glentruim was built. Being built on a hill, no doubt a piece of land was flattened to construct the foundations of Glentruim. Also, more than likely, it would have been the knoll where the Macphersons retreated. It would, therefore, not be unreasonable to speculate that the said hill would at that time have passed through our bedroom. I had no doubt in my mind that this was what had happened, and it was the spirits of the Macphersons that had raged through our bedroom that night, as they did from the top of the knoll in 1386. Euan, who found it difficult to understand the unexplained, was more sceptical.

# 8

# *A Son and Heir*

I suffered yet another difficult pregnancy with Lachlan, our son. With one child already and a business to run, it was not practical to take the advice of doctors and rest. A miscarriage inevitably threatened. I decided to go to Perth Royal Infirmary, because I did not know any of the gynaecologists in Raigmore Hospital in Inverness. I also wished to be close to my parents, who lived seven miles away from Perth.

I was admitted to a ward which had eight beds. A few of the young girls in the ward were there to have abortions, which further upset my already fragile emotional state. I had nothing in common with any of these patients and became withdrawn and tearful. The ward was busy and noisy, not compatible with the recommendations given to me by my doctor for 'peace and rest'.

My first miscarriage, before I had had Catriona, had left me traumatised for weeks afterwards. I had cried every time I saw another baby or heard news of a friend giving birth. I had envied my contemporaries who already had children, and had feared that I would never be blessed with children myself.

It had taken a few years for me to conceive in the first place, a difficulty I had put down to being left weak after contracting hepatitis. This had occurred in 1969, the year after we married, when I had been barrier-nursing a gentleman at the renal dialysis unit in the Royal Infirmary of Edinburgh. After his death, I had put the needles, blades and waste from his room into a thick green bag, pushed them through the hatch, then de-gowned. I had then removed the bags from the other side of the hatch, accidentally pricking myself in the process with a discarded needle in one of them. Because I had been on night-duty when this incident happened, I had had to wait a day and a night to receive the antidote. This was too late for me, the virus having already infected my system. I became very ill, but because at that time we were living in our cottage on the south side of Edinburgh, which had coom ceilings in the bedroom and therefore was rather dark, my doctor had not noticed how jaundiced I had become. By the time I was taken into hospital I was almost unconscious. The doctor on duty in the Accident and Emergency Department happened to be one of a team working in the same unit as myself and he immediately gave me an injection to stop the vomiting and retching. But unfortunately, my liver had already been damaged and the drug pushed me into deep unconsciousness, since my liver was unable to absorb it. At this stage I became critically ill.

I was in hospital for weeks and was lucky to survive. Sadly one of the doctors on my team and a biochemist who had been dealing with blood from the same deceased gentleman had both also contracted hepatitis and subsequently died.

Gloves were then introduced universally for all staff who handled blood and body fluids. It took two years for me to be completely clear of infection and really well again. This incident was widely publicised at the time, and was later the subject of a book by one of the doctors at the Edinburgh Royal Infirmary.

Eventually I recovered, and by the time Lachlan was due I assumed that all medical traumas were behind me. This was not to be, for in the ward at Perth Royal Infirmary, old wounds were reopened. I was subjected to the usual tests and examinations, followed by an agonising wait for the results, which I kept Euan up-to-date with whenever I managed to bag the well-used telephone trolley in the ward. On about the third day the consultant, a friend of my father, came to do his rounds. I wondered which century he had come out of as he stood at the bottom of each bed, his medical retinue clearly full of admiration for this god-like figure of authority. No confidentiality was respected here. The consultant spoke in a loud, pompous voice, telling each patient exactly what the results of their tests were and what was to be their fate. Within the silence insisted upon by the ward sister, we were all soon to know every private detail about each other, as we sat propped up in our meticulously tidied beds.

It came to my turn. I felt that I was a number, not a person. The consultant was cold, insensitive and rude. As he flicked through his notes he informed his awestruck followers: 'This woman's baby is dead; she will be on the list for theatre tomorrow.' He then moved on with his entourage. I was left shocked and extremely angry that I should be treated so callously.

Instinctively I knew my baby was not dead, despite the opinion of the specialists, whom I should have been able to trust. To a young approachable trainee doctor who came round later that evening I expressed my concerns, telling him that I really did not think that I had lost the baby. I then telephoned Euan before crying myself to sleep.

Late that evening I was awoken by the young trainee. Having read through the ward records, he had found a serious error: the notes of another Macpherson, a day patient, had been confused with mine. My baby was alive. Late as it was, I again telephoned Euan, who arrived first thing the next morning to take me home.

In preparation for the imminent birth of Lachlan, I went to stay with my best friend, Vicky Thain, and her husband, Tony, in Edinburgh. The gynaecologist present at Catriona's birth had agreed to deliver my next baby, so it was to Edinburgh I had to return. Vicky and I had known each other for most of our lives, beginning with our school days at Kilgraston, in Bridge of Earn. Because we had shared all of our problems in life and knew absolutely everything about each other, our friendship was very special. When I had stayed at the Thains' before Catriona was born, Vicky and I had each been expecting our first child. Consequently, when we arrived by taxi in the early hours of the morning at the Simpson Maternity Unit, the staff must have presumed that they had to book two labour rooms! Vicky had to say a great many times, when approached by a nurse, 'It's not me – it's my friend who is in labour!'

Not many hours before Lachlan was born, I had been enjoying a Chinese take-away with Vicky and Tony, sitting on the floor, a plate balanced on the 'bump'. I had realised that I was about to go into labour, but a take-away was such a novelty to me after living in the north, isolated from such treats, that I finished my meal before saying a word. Lachlan was born a short time later in the Western General Hospital. He was the baby I might not have had, had I not questioned the diagnosis given to me by the consultant in Perth. He was very precious, and I was extremely lucky to have him at all.

Euan had brought Catriona to see me and her new brother in hospital at the weekend, a visit I remember as if it were yesterday. She sat on my bed wearing her Sunday best, skirt and cape, both in the ancient red Macpherson tartan. She was only two years old and most well-behaved considering what a tiring, tedious journey she must have had. Apparently she later slept all the way home to Glentruim, but when she awoke on the way up the front drive burst into tears and cried, 'Oh Mummy, Mummy, Mummy!'

Once again I returned from hospital to a welcome-home party. I was taken aback by the presence of The Sparrow, who had chosen to accept the invitation from Euan, just as she had done for Catriona's arrival. It was for these two occasions only that she relented and stepped back into Glentruim, the place to which she had vowed never to return.

Catriona, accustomed to being the centre of attention, found it all too much. My efforts to make her feel just as important as her demanding baby brother were of no use, and as I held her in my arms, she scratched me down the face. Catriona's nose, interestingly, was not the only one out of joint. When Euan remarked, 'I'm not surprised', after this incident, I came to realise how sidelined a father can feel at the birth of a new child.

Lachlan was the youngest in his year when he started at Gergask School in Laggan. The school had recently progressed from one to two teachers, having increased its intake to the grand total of about twenty children. Here was provided the best start to life you could ever wish for. There was undivided attention and a pace suited to each child's abilities. Isobel Geddes was the head teacher, whose excellent and capable guidance encouraged both parent and community involvement in the school. It was, however, the first position after college for the young second teacher, Iona Gallacher, who learned readily in the happy, enlightened environment of Gergask.

Isobel was the sort of person who managed to get everyone together for school functions and her enthusiasm for drama, poetry, music and dance spilled over to the children and their families. Everyone in the area would participate in the school activities in some way or another. When a school play or concert was due, mothers would bake for days and fathers would help prepare the village hall. Every performance by the children of Laggan would be yet another important stage in the process of their education. The pupils of Laggan were entered for the Festival of Music and Verse in Kingussie every year and, among them, there were sure to be successful candidates; they gained first and second prizes in their competition classes. Such recognition of their prowess was a deserved tribute to their teachers and parents, but mostly to the enthusiasm and team spirit of the children themselves.

I would chat with Isobel over a cup of coffee, reminiscing about the shows she had produced in the village hall. The dramatised song 'The Wee Kirkcudbright Centipede' was one that particularly stayed in our minds. All the children had been made up into a centipede by forming a long chain, in sequence according to their height. They had to put their arms around each other's waists, their legs close behind the person in front. Lachlan, being the smallest, was at the tail. As the centipede wriggled around in dance, Lachlan's tiny feet were out of step, which meant he was dragged across the platform as he gripped the shirt of the boy in front of him. This entire display of dance, which should have been perfect and precise, turned into a comedy because of the tail of the centipede! There was a full and sympathetic audience in the hall including mothers, fathers, grandparents and many local worthies. Our local pharmacist, Jean Scobbie, herself no mean performer and patron of the arts, asked, 'Who's that wee "cratur" at the tail?' On being told it was Lachlan Macpherson from Glentruim, Jean nodded, laughed and said, 'Ah – the wee Laird.'

Lachlan was a sensitive child and I remember him saying to me when he was barely stringing his words together, as we waited for the school car to pick up Catriona at the telephone box past Breakachy, 'Do you remember when I was an old man and lived in the little cottage by the sea?' I thought then what an extraordinary remark, which surely came from something in his 'past life'! He was also an endearing child, very shy and totally dependent on his older sister. Given that he was so small and the youngest, he was almost over-protected by all in the school. But he was also clumsy. If you positioned an object in the middle of the floor and asked him to avoid it, he would be sure to bump into it. At that time in the school it was decided to convert a broad step, which led to the 'wee room', into a safe slope. This would help in moving furniture from room to room, especially the well-used piano. It was also hoped that it would assist in making Lachlan's daily entry a bit more dignified! Lachlan still tripped in each morning and was subsequently nicknamed

Mr MacFeet. The new name had only just been applied when the phone rang and the phone-duty pupil answered it. 'Excuse me, Mrs Geddes. Mr McFeat from the office in Inverness would like a word with you.' After a second of disbelief the children and staff shared one of their many moments of laughter together. To this day Mr MacFeat in Inverness must wonder why his name caused such amusement.

After various incidents resulting from this poor coordination, such as being stuck in the back of chairs, it was suggested that Lachlan should see a child psychologist. We sat in the smoking-room, where uncomfortable meetings had taken place before. The psychologist's assessment of Lachlan was followed by a serious discussion, during which he told us that our son had left-eye dominance. Many people have this condition but go through life unaware of it. The psychologist further added, when prompted, that university would be unsuitable for Lachlan and that he would be fortunate to achieve standard grades. I found it unforgivable to label a child in this way, and we had to live with this sentence for years until we found out otherwise. Although he had not done particularly well at his preparatory school in Pitlochry, where, much to our disgust, he was labelled a 'reject' because his coordination was not accurate enough for him to be in the cricket team, he later proved the psychologist utterly wrong. After attending Glenalmond College in Perthshire, Lachlan excelled in his studies and later became involved in computer technology.

Looking back, I think about the terrible things we do to our children for the sake of what we perceive to be the best education. At the age of eight, I had felt that Lachlan was far too young to go to boarding school. How he hated being torn away from home on a Sunday evening. Lachlan summed it up nicely one day as we motored down the drive to take him back to school, tears rolling down his little cheeks. 'Have you left anything behind this time?' his father enquired from behind the driving wheel. 'Yes,' whispered Lachlan. Slamming his foot on the brake, Euan then asked what it was he had left behind. 'My happiness,' this eight-year-old meekly replied, choking on his tears. The journey was completed in a miserable silence. Both Catriona and Lachlan started boarding school the same year, Catriona at Kilgraston, where I was educated. This left a big void in my life and I was as unhappy as they were.

A friend suggested that Lachlan should take something to school that was part of home, and so made him a beautiful oak tuck-box, with brass handle and hinges. I do believe that Lachlan considered that this box was a part of home; it was kept locked and crammed with everything that was precious to him, including his tuck.

I did, however, have just one more pregnancy, when Catriona was five and Lachlan was two, but it met with misfortune. On the way home from a shopping expedition to Inverness there was a fierce snow storm. It was difficult to judge the width of road, with no white lines in the middle and the snow banking up on the verges. The ditches on either side of the back road to Glentruim were completely submerged. With virtually no visibility and a blizzard howling round us, our vehicle landed in a ditch. Euan went for assistance, but so extreme was the cold it was essential that I got the children home. The mile-long driveway seemed endless, snow and wind hammering our faces, forcing our eyes to shut as we were subjected to a severe weather-beating.

We struggled, how we struggled, up the drive in those arctic conditions. The trees either side of the avenue were laden with snow, and walking became more strenuous as snow thickened underfoot. Catriona's little feet could hardly keep up as I dragged her along by the hand and she has never let me forget what I kept saying to her that afternoon: 'If we stop, we die.' Lachlan was heavy in my arms and by then, like the other two of us, miserable with the cold. In his fear and frustration he pulled at one of my ear-rings, which tore through the lobe of my ear and was lost forever in the snow. The least of my problems, I thought at the time.

The long haul to reach home left us numb with cold, our limbs stiff and white. I left the children in their outer clothes in the boudoir, put on an electric heater and went to the back door to fetch wood and coal. First I intended to fetch a bucket of coal, which would give out a stronger heat than wood. With no feeling in either my fingers or my toes, I lost my balance while carrying the coal-bucket and tripped down the back steps. Whether it was the fall, the severe conditions or the carrying of a heavy child up the avenue, I will never know, but this triggered my final miscarriage.

Because we lived so far north, we were accustomed to days of fighting against the elements during the severe winters. Another of the treacherous journeys I had to make followed a mid-morning summons made by the school to collect the children immediately. The weather was closing in rapidly with fast-falling snow, the winds rising. Down the back road I went in the Land Rover, with visibility so poor that it was impossible to see the road except through memory. I turned the Land Rover over in a ditch. Shaken and frozen, I then ventured on by foot, over a mile to our neighbouring farm at Breakachy. My only guides were the tops of the fence posts, which I clutched hand over hand until I reached the farm. Blue with cold, I felt the beginning of frostbite in my fingers and toes. I must have had at least six inches of snow clinging to the top of my woolly hat – what a sight for Campbell Slimon when he opened the farm door! He took me back to the Land Rover in his tractor, and pulled it out of the ditch for me, but his good deed was not complete until he had escorted me to the end of the back road. I then made the rest of the journey alone, very gingerly. Although the school had long closed, I found the children with Isobel Geddes in the school-house, snug and well in front of an open fire. It was late afternoon before we got home, having had to travel along the main road into Newtonmore then back up the A9 to Glentruim. Getting straight into a hot bath, I was still cold, but at least we had all safely returned.

Perhaps these treacherous journeys could be considered one of the negative aspects to living in the country, the local school being some distance away. But the advantages of a country village school far outnumbered any of the inconveniences experienced. Laggan, which was a small village where everyone knew everything about everyone else, had its good points and bad, as in any other rural community. Yet, if someone was in need of assistance, everyone would rally round. One old resident, who awoke early each day, kept a careful note of every puff of smoke as it rose from the chimneys of the village, just to see that everyone was alive! This behaviour may have seemed nosey, but it was only a sign of concern for the well-being of neighbours. People did and do look out for each other in Laggan.

Above all, the school children benefited the most from this safe environment. Their education was wide and varied, and their imaginative play was an important factor in the process of growing-up. In the bicycle shed were four old 'all-in-one' desks, which would be put to use for children's games. When there were thick falls of snow the children would turn the desks upside-down and use them as sleighs! I was amused to learn that Lachlan was once found kissing his only female classmate behind that particular shed! Times had somewhat changed since his father's school days: no-one now bothered a bit!

While at Gergask, Catriona was described by Isobel as having a 'quiet application' to her work and a love of language, attributes to be encouraged. Catriona was a deep thinker and, like her father, later read psychology at university. She worked hard at school, but also very much enjoyed her imaginative games with her classmates at Gergask. The play surrounding the stone houses was often talked about by her and her friends. On the other side of the wall, beyond the school boundary, was a large field in which the children were allowed to play, by kind permission of the Gaskbeg farmer. They shared the field with cattle, sheep and, of course, cow-pats! It was here, during their breaks, that they built a village of 'stone houses', which were made by laying large stones on the ground, the different rooms divided by other stones. In these imaginary houses gaps were left for front doors, and also for internal ones between each room. All the rooms had furniture and belongings in the form of smaller, suitably-shaped stones, with rushes on the floors in the bedrooms for beds. Pebbles from the river were used to buy things from the 'stone shop', and there was even a 'stone pub'! Frequently civil disputes were settled in what would now be called circle-time, or personal and social development. On one occasion someone stole a 'stone telephone' from another child's stone house. During the submission of evidence, one earnest little girl divulged all. Maintaining her role, she stated that she had been the shopkeeper, and had seen the whole episode from her window. Such was the degree of imagination enjoyed during play!

The children's play was simple, yet a sound background for the future development of their minds. Children came and left Gergask, but nevertheless those stone houses were spoken about long after primary-school days. The farmer's field, used for decades, is now sadly out of bounds because of the stringent health and safety regulations. It almost seems that in present times the cultivation of imagination is also out of bounds.

# 9

# *The Community*

BETWEEN the births of Catriona and Lachlan, Euan at last joined me at Glentruim, having given up his job in Edinburgh. He started anew as Principle Psychologist at the Raigmore Hospital, Inverness. This was what we had both been longing for; I felt alone and frightened no longer. Weekends had never given us enough time together, even when Euan occasionally came back on a Thursday instead of a Friday. One of these Thursdays, when Euan returned home unexpectedly, we had unwelcome visitors, whom I would not have easily handled by myself. He had returned home 'Highland' style, wearing his kilt. That evening I was locking all the outside doors for the night when I noticed three men creeping up to the back door. I shouted for Euan, who grabbed a Lochaber axe off the wall in the front hall and ran through the back corridors, brandishing the long pole firmly in his hands. His cry must have been similar to those of his warrior-ancestors during battle as he confronted the intruders on the back door-step. They fled down the drive as if they had seen a ghost!

When Euan worked in Inverness, he had to leave very early and return equally late. He drove up and down to Raigmore every day on the notoriously treacherous old A9 for several years, before eventually deciding to take the train. Sometimes I would drive him to the railway station and then return to pick him up after work in the evening. Since the local dairy would not deliver to Glentruim, I had made a deal with them that we should collect our milk at the railway station every day. When the children first went to primary school and were asked during class, 'Where do you get your milk from?' they would say with great conviction, 'The railway station!'

I was accustomed to getting up early, but Euan was a night-owl, as he used to say, who preferred to spend more time awake at the other end of the day. I often gave him breakfast in bed knowing that it was a bad time of the day for him. On one such morning, I remember going upstairs with his breakfast tray and opening the door to find two enormous eyes looking down on me from the top of the wardrobe. I had heard a rustling sound in the chimney during the night, but when it stopped I had not given it any more thought. Then, at this early hour in the morning, I stood staring into the large brown eyes of a tawny owl. I dumped the tray at Euan's side of the bed, quickly opened the curtains and then the window as wide as I could. 'Here's your breakfast,' I said, 'and, by the way, there's an owl on top of the wardrobe.' I left Euan with this predicament and sped out of the room, shutting the door behind me! Euan sleepily ate his breakfast, quite unperturbed by the fluttering of the owl as it found its way out of the window and back into the cool open air again.

Another morning I had let our two retrievers out into the garden and gone back inside the house to prepare breakfast. When I called the dogs back in, all I could see was a few of my hens running around in panic, totally denuded of feathers. They had been stripped by the dogs. It was a horrible sight and they were all dying, bar one. I took this last casualty into the kitchen, placing it in a dark corner by the Welsh dresser where, before making its last sad little screech, it laid an egg! Up I went to Euan with his breakfast tray, stating, 'You have a very fresh egg this morning!'

Now that Euan was at home, we began to market the shooting

and fishing on the estate. We started with sportsmen from throughout Britain, who lodged with us at Glentruim, later also receiving clients from abroad. If Euan was ill, I had to manage the guests as best I could. Some guests, however, particularly from France, were not easy to control. I had an awkward time with a party from Paris while Euan was in bed with influenza. Because the men were continually hanging their sodden garments over priceless antique furniture in their bedrooms, I firmly told them that they should give me their damp clothes to hang up by the boiler, in the butler's pantry, as soon as they came back from a wet day's shooting. Not waiting until they got to their rooms, they obediently stripped in the hall, much to the amusement of my mother, who was staying that week. Through her laughter she managed to exclaim, 'Oh la la! C'est la Folie Bergere!'

Soon I became very involved with the local community and was invited onto several local committees, which was a good way to get to know people in the district. I began to enjoy my new life at Glentruim.

My nursing background came into use when I was asked to join the Local Health Council, and at that time I also became a member of the Highland Children's Panel. Later, a group of us in Badenoch and Strathspey were involved in the task of purchasing and establishing the Highland Hospice in Inverness. There were about thirty people in all at the first meeting held at Glentruim, which included the local doctor, the headmaster of Newtonmore Primary School and the local minister. We had held a 'Daffodil Tea Party' the day before in aid of a local charity and so, to save me searching for chairs, I brought in the wooden benches which had been used for the occasion. I was told that they were most uncomfortable, as indeed they were, so the meeting was conducted as quickly as possible so that the refreshments could be dispensed, not including tea!

The most time-consuming of all the organisations I was involved in was the Wild Cat Committee. This was set up in order to persuade tourists to visit local villages through which the old A9 had passed, and which were now bypassed by the recently constructed new A9. It was a great source of worry to all shop-keepers and businessmen that this diversion of most of the traffic would have a severe effect on local trade. Jack Richmond, a retired forester from Newtonmore, was the instigator of the Wild Cat Committee, which was extremely well-supported by a great many people who were prepared to work tirelessly in organising events throughout each summer. Jack was a remarkable person, totally dedicated to the survival of Newtonmore, Laggan and Dalwhinnie, the villages which were on the boundaries of the Wild Cat area. Jack had been paraplegic since he was eighteen years old, following an accident: a tree had fallen on top of him, breaking his back. His disabilities never hindered him from promoting our villages, which he did extremely successfully. It is thanks to him that the Wild Cat area is so well-known today.

As a member of the Badenoch Committee, I held a large event at Glentruim and Jack generously paid for a whisky-tasting, which was undertaken by Allan Keegan. This was in 1984, when an Interskola group visited Scotland. My event coincided with their post-conference weekend. Participating were teachers and educators from most of the northern European countries. They had been promised a cultural experience, hosted and organised by Donald MacDonald, headmaster of Newtonmore Primary School. He had invited along the celebrated John MacDougal, a champion piper and his Highland Council piping instructor. Donald asked John to play a piobaireachd (the classical music of the Scottish bagpipe) during the evening. Euan thought that this was far too high-brow for these guests, but it was nevertheless played. Donald introduced the piece, gave the background to the composition and pointed out to the visitors what to listen for. It was called, 'I got a Kiss of the King's Hand', and was very much enjoyed by everyone. Euan had to admit that it had been a good choice. The evening's entertainment took place during a warm summer's night, with several local performers and a traditional dinner provided by ourselves. Afterwards I was persuaded to play the clarsach. The foreign guests left with warm hearts and fond memories of their Highland evening and dinner at Glentruim.

Since Glentruim proved an excellent venue for barbeques, during that same summer we opened the gardens in aid of the Wild Cat cause. Posters were put up throughout the valley advertising the occasion, with admission £1.00 for adults and 50p for children and senior citizens. The posters claimed that there would be 'Pony Rides, Clay Pigeon Shooting, Archery, a Treasure Hunt, Hoopla, a Raffle, Produce Stall, Bric-a-Brac, and Cake Stall'. We even had a drinks licence! It was advertised as 'An Evening's Enjoyment in a Very Special Setting'. For a fund-raising event such as this there was sure to be support from the locals. Alaister Thompson, who then owned and ran the Gask-more Hotel in Laggan, was always the first to offer his services and would be busy putting up trestle tables and working at any other jobs required long before other helpers arrived. He would assist anyone with anything, from cutting grass or chopping wood to general repairs. He was a local character with a patch over one eye, but unfortunately he died young, following a heart attack. Typical of Alaister, right to the end, he had been obliging a friend and was mending his roof at the time of his sudden death.

Not only did I have the honour of working with Jack Richmond on the Wild Cat committees, organising events, but I also joined him at trade fairs. At these we would promote many organisations, businesses, hotels and country houses, which included the Glentruim estate. We would have large boards with pictures of the trades at the back of the stand and would offer shortbread and a unique liqueur concoction to entice our customers to read our literature. The strength of the drink offered depended on our generosity with the whisky; honey, the other ingredient, was then added. This mixture was made up by us under the table! In 1989 Jack, his wife Hettie and daughter

Yvonne marketed and developed this concoction as a modern liqueur. It is now known as 'Stags Breath' and contains fine whisky and fermented comb heather honey! It was named after one of the whisky brands in Compton MacKenzie's novel, *Whisky Galore*, and below the picture on its label it reads: 'These are the clan lands of the Macphersons and their war-cry hill, Craig Dhu, commands the neighbourhood.'

Through the work of the Wild Cat committee, Hogmanay was introduced as a major tourist attraction in Newtonmore. Before midnight there would be a march through the village to the village square, led by a notable pipe band; then precisely at midnight there would be firing of guns. Amongst the cheers and strong voices singing 'Auld Lang Syne', Walker's shortbread and 'Stags Breath' would be handed out and glasses would be raised, toasting all and sundry. Then there was dancing into the early hours of the next day with much fun and carefree laughter.

While the new A9 was being constructed, dumper-trucks were brought over from Russia, massive vehicles but ideal for the job. We were asked to host a special banquet at Glentruim for the Russian diplomats who came over at that time, and it was all to be kept very secret. They were the most attractive people, fluent in English and extremely polite. They arrived in a bus along with their bodyguards, who patrolled the grounds throughout the evening. The banquet consisted of every available kind of game and fish, and the Russians complemented the feast with crates of vodka and other spirits. It was highly successful, but a long and tiring evening which was not helped at the end when I found our housekeeper intoxicated in her sitting-room, having consumed a whole bottle of vodka. I could tell that she had been tippling when she was serving at dinner. As the evening wore on, I noticed that her bright red lipstick had been applied further and further up from her mouth each time I saw her!

That same year, while the dumper-trucks were working on the

new road, the winter was extremely severe and we were snowed up for about ten days. It was the year that all farmers were asked to make crosses in the snow if they required fodder to be dropped by helicopters for their livestock. As we had winter grazing and were looking after sheep, many of which became stranded in the snow, we too had to make crosses in the bottom fields, like many other farmers in the valley. Some outlying areas could be reached by the Snow-Tric, which was a motor vehicle equipped for these conditions, but when the snow fell more heavily, reaching over the fence-posts, we had to wear snowshoes. I remember walking over the top of the fence-posts across the snow to reach the main road, just to see if I could spot life! I saw none. Soon we were without either electricity or telephone facilities. We had large drums of flour in the basement, the freezers were full, and I had also taken the precaution of covering the freezers with quantities of newspaper and blankets to keep the food frozen as long as possible. We were not worried, for we had enough provisions to sustain us for weeks. The days were short and we lit paraffin lamps once darkness fell, sat by log fires and boiled up water on the old range for our hot-water bottles.

The snow had risen halfway up the front door, but we had continued to dig ourselves out every day, not really making much progress, only as far as the conservatory. With the snow that we had dug out we helped the children to make an igloo, which must have made that winter one of their most memorable!

At the end of the ten days, just as we were all extending the igloo, we heard the sound of a high-pitched engine. Suddenly, at the corner of the avenue, we could see a big dumper-truck sweeping up the drive, snow being pushed to the sides with no effort at all. It was clearing in seconds what we had taken ten days to achieve with shovels!

That moment was both exciting and sad – exciting to see other human beings, yet sad to lose our peaceful isolation. The police came too, for as they had been unable to contact us, they wished to make sure that we were all safe and well. This was very reassuring.

When the work on the new A9 started again and was then finally completed, we were invited to see it before the official opening. We all had a ride on the dumper-trucks and the road seemed large and spacious in comparison with the old one. This was the new road through the Highlands, a road welcomed by the travellers but dreaded by the local traders for fear of forgotten villages and dwindling trade.

After a few years, once we had established friendships with many of the local people, we would hold a large New Year's party at Glentruim, which was an ideal venue for us. Firstly, we did not have to arrange babysitters, and secondly, we could enjoy a drink! Latterly, however, Allan and Marjorie Macpherson-Fletcher, who had become very good friends of ours, began to hold this celebration at Balavil on alternate years to ours. New Year in the Highlands would stretch into many more days than the normal public holiday!

Marjorie had lost her first husband in a traffic accident in 1975, leaving her with three children. She then married Allan, who inherited Balavil from his Aunt Peggy, and they then had two more children together. 'Aunt Peggy', as we all fondly called her, was a great character and could be seen taking her constitutional daily walk along the old A9 every morning with a bonnet on her head.

The New Year party which I remember most at Balavil was the one when, after much drinking and frivolity, we all decided to 'first-foot' two of their workers on the estate. At that time Allan and Marjorie were living in their farmhouse, the big house being tenanted. There was thick snow on the ground, and, feeling no chill because of our host's generosity with the drams, Allan and Marjorie, along with Allan's sister and her husband as well as

Euan and myself, set forth with sleighs. The purpose of the sleighs was to carry those with high-heels! We were off to visit Jockie and Jeanie Milton, who lived in a little cottage down by the railway. 'A Happy New Year', rang out from us all as we handed over the traditional piece of coal and a bottle of whisky. We had not long settled before a roaring fire when Jeannie fetched her melodeon and Jockie began to sing. Euan impressed us all by singing along with him, in what was presumed to be Gaelic. The Miltons were thrilled to have a Gaelic speaker joining in so vocally and, as they expressed their pleasure, Marjorie turned to me and said, 'I didn't know Euan could speak Gaelic!' 'He can't,' I replied, as bemused as she was. It was of course that time of year, one heard what one wished and obviously everyone, full of the right kind of spirit, thought that Euan had sung in the native tongue! We returned home to Glentruim in the early hours of the next day and according to Allan and Marjorie, we took their farm gates with us! Our Range Rover had somehow damaged the gates as we passed through them on our way home!

Our life in the north was becoming richer with friends and busier as the days went by, both with work and entertainment. However, this was the way of life in the Highlands; living in the country meant hard work, and times of leisure were of our own making.

# 10

# *Touch not a Cat bot a Glove*

IF you travel to Fort William from Glentruim, towards Loch Laggan, you happen to come across the impressive sight of Ardverikie, sitting on the far banks of Loch Laggan. This magnificent house has been used recently for the filming of *Monarch of the Glen*. The television series has not only given much pleasure to those who have been avid followers of the story but also to those living locally, who have been very much involved. It has also brought interest and acclaim to the area. The name Ardverikie is derived from the Gaelic, Ard-mheirgidh – The Height of the Standard. This was the place where Queen Victoria and Prince Albert stayed from 21 August to 17 September 1847 and, since there was no bridge there in those days, they were rowed across the loch. They used it as a Highland Retreat, Prince Albert spending his days shooting while Queen Victoria fished. Queen Victoria had found the place beautiful and wild, but unfortunately the weather was dreadful while she was there, with a great deal of rain. It is said that if the weather had not been so foul, then perhaps she would have bought Ardverikie rather than Balmoral. I believe that it was also thought that the midges put her off! Later, in 1871, Ardverikie was burned down and then rebuilt in 1873, only to be destroyed once again by fire just before it was completed.

The new house was designed by John Rhind and built for Sir John Ramsden in 1874–79. A tower, which had been added on to the old building, was incorporated into the new design with the consequence that, when the mist is low, it looks like a fairy-tale castle sitting in the clouds. Ardverikie is of further historical interest, for within its grounds lies the grave of King Fergus. Moreover, it is claimed that six other Scottish monarchs are buried there.

A Highlander can bear a grudge for all his days and Euan was no exception. He would never set foot in Ardverikie and I always wondered why, until one day he told me. Ardverikie and its surrounding land used to be part of Cluny estate, owned by Cluny Macpherson. In 1844, when Cluny ran out of money, he let Ardverikie on a long lease to the Marquis of Abercorn, and it was then that the estate was put at the disposal of the royal family. In 1869, however, Ardverikie was rented to Sir John Ramsden, a wealthy man from Huddersfield, and a condition of the lease was that when the tenure ended, Cluny would have to compensate for any improvements made, which included the planting of trees. It was reputed that Sir John Ramsden spent money on the estate 'like well water', as described by an old man of Laggan. Sir John was a wealthy man and spent in the region of £180,000, mainly on planting trees. There was no prospect of Cluny making redemption, and so the ownership of Ardverikie was handed over to Sir John. Ardverikie thus fell out of Macpherson hands after a great many years, a sad loss to the family. Each time Euan passed Ardverikie, when driving from Glentruim to Fort William, he always remembered this tale.

In much more recent years *The Missionary* was filmed at Ardverikie and one of the lead actors was Trevor Howard. He and Euan had become friends over the years, having met on the road coming north from the Lake District. At that time Euan was still a student at Edinburgh University and had been in the Lake District rock-climbing, one of his favourite pastimes. Euan had been hitch-hiking there and back, as students did quite safely in those days. It was only after chatting for quite some time that

Euan recognised his driver, who, to his surprise, turned out to be Trevor Howard. Euan later told me that they had had a very interesting conversation on the long journey back to Edinburgh.

Because we could not reach Trevor by telephone, I was the one who had to go to Ardverikie to invite him to dinner. As I passed the little lodge and drove over the bridge to the castle I remembered the circumstances which led to Ardverikie's being taken out of Macpherson hands, an injustice which Euan continued to feel on behalf of the Cluny Macphersons. Euan lived up to the Macpherson motto, 'Touch not a cat bot a glove' – do not cross a Macpherson! He did not easily forget and forgive.

Trevor was so pleased to be asked to dinner and said that it could be monotonous and dreary having to return to the hotel each night after filming. Filming dragged on the evening he was meant to come to dinner and he had to cancel the engagement. We never saw him again.

Ardverikie Castle is in itself a picture, but its beauty is compounded by the splendid loch which lies before it. The loch has lovely beaches and during the holidays I would take the children down to the lochside and let them play on the sands. This was also the venue for many a village school outing or sports day – a children's paradise, if blessed with good weather. However, as a family we never did go into the castle.

One day, long ago, when the water in Loch Laggan had dropped and the sands lay bare, a film crew went there to record an agricultural programme. The subject to be covered was 'The Dying of a Glen'. Because our own glen was still so vibrant, the interviewers were gathering information on the reasons why we had managed to have such a healthy survival. John Duncan, one of the old inhabitants of the area was heard to say, 'Such a pity you came today when the tide's out.' This was the humour of the Laggan people.

In the Macphersons' past, there was not only sadness through loss of land, but also grief through personal loss, such as in the life of Euan's Aunt Eva. It was a story very much in my thoughts when I first settled at Glentruim.

When you find yourself running a house that has had customs and rules stringently followed for over a century, with very little change even to minor details such as the use of the rooms or the positioning of the furniture, it takes time before you become aware that all may not be to your liking, and also before you ultimately dare to consider change. One of the bedrooms, the only one with central heating, was usually kept for guests. It was large and airy in its own corridor, with a bathroom next door. Both of these rooms were north-facing, with a view across the valley, and it took us a while to realise that it was the obvious choice for a master bedroom. So we then persuaded ourselves to move into it. I liked the bedroom; it was very comfortable and I loved to look out of the window first thing in the morning, when, in stolen seconds, I would find myself looking down through cloud and mist to discover the colours and shapes of an artist's dream. There was something very special about such a calm, striking scene that could be caught only momentarily by the person fortunate enough to be there at the time. It was pleasant over by the window, which had an awkward tubular radiator beneath it, and so sometimes in the morning I would take advantage of both the view and the remaining warmth, settling myself there for a short time to ponder a little over the history related to me about Euan's family. It was during our first few weeks in this bedroom that I gave a lot of thought to the sad life of Euan's Aunt Eva.

Born in 1882, Eva had lived at Glentruim along with her sister and four brothers, one of whom was Euan's father. According to the older members of the community and indeed to everyone who knew her, she was an incredibly beautiful girl and greatly admired. She was described as always being bright and cheerful with an abundance of energy, who would often be seen riding into the village on her bicycle. With her long auburn hair neatly piled up on top of her head, and the feminine mutton chop sleeves that were so often her style of dress, she caused many a head to turn as she quietly pedalled past the daily shoppers.

Poor Eva, her life became full of anguish. Like many of her unlucky young contemporaries, the hopes and dreams of her amour were abruptly halted by events of the First World War. Her young man never came back and she was left alone to pick up the threads of life and to live it the best way that she could, alone for the rest of her days.

The next cruel blow to her life came when Eva's brother Duncan married. She had to leave her cherished home – there was only room for one Lady of the House. Glentruim held as large a part of her heart as did her brave young soldier, and so living for her became almost too much to bear from that day onwards.

Eva was not completely destitute because her father had left her a legacy, with which she managed to buy herself a little house in Lynchat, three miles north of Kingussie, with ample money left over to live on. For a time she survived on the interest from that sum, which, if managed correctly, would have seen her quite nicely through all her days. But, as time went on, she felt her losses to be increasingly intolerable. In her wretched state of mind she sought escape through, as it could be said, the curse of alcohol. Gradually all the money was squandered and eventually even her capital had to be realised. It was then only a matter of time before her house had to be sold to provide her with the drink that had become her addiction.

Taking a room in the village of Newtonmore, there was now less distance between her abode and her place of childhood. How she longed to return home and how it tormented her latterly to see her brother's widow in the place that she thought should rightly have been hers. The bitterness was like a cancer to her, preying deeply on her mind. She felt that there was an outsider running her home, living in the lap of luxury, while she had to demean herself by finding some kind of employment to keep solvent. A lady of her status would never have dreamt of being trained to do anything but run a household of servants, so what chances did Eva have in the outside world? What courage she certainly showed when, totally degraded, she dug the gardens of any needful villager who would be kind enough to give her work.

After one of her long, tiring days of manual labour, while cutting her toenails, she accidentally cut into the quick. The toe became infected and the infection soon spread up into her leg, which finally led to her death from gangrene. Eva's miserable days ended, at last releasing her from her hard, tormented life.

Since moving into that particular bedroom, Eva had been perpetually in my mind. It was the room Katie had occupied and subsequently died in, and though I had never felt her presence, there were recurring and unexplained oddities. I would be deeply asleep then woken by footsteps coming into the room during the early hours of the morning. Instinctively I would call out, 'Who is it?' expecting an answer, but none would ever come. These footsteps seemed to come in, pause at the side of the bed, then go out again, gradually fading away along the corridor.

One morning, as I was opening the curtains and looking out at the last moments of the pink sunrise, I noticed a solitary gull on the front lawn. It was pure white and was standing there quite still, as if waiting for the household to awaken. I woke Euan and then we both watched it as it paced up and down across the top terrace of the lawn until the full light of morning came. Then it flew away. For a week or so this gull returned each morning, until we began to feel that it was part of the family – a message from the past. Ready to welcome each day in with us, it would stand patiently until we opened the curtains; then the morning walk would begin.

Just before dawn one morning, I followed the sound of footsteps down the corridor. For a brief moment they stopped before the door which divided the main bedrooms from the children's, but I was aware they had not deserted me. The three narrow steps to the right led to the room under the tower and in front of its door was another small, bevelled door leading to the tower itself. When the sound of footsteps returned, I followed them up the winding staircase to the first rounded room. I felt as if I were floating, as if being blown along by the wind. This little room could only house a tiny child's brass bed, a table and a white wicker chair. The entrance door was moulded into the round room, as was the one on the other side. Turning the little brass door-handle on the second door, I went up the spiral staircase and through a similar room in which there was a writing-desk, chair and Tilly lamp. Both of these rooms had windows on three sides with splendid views all around. The final staircase led to the bolted door to the parapets. Having unbolted top and bottom stiff, rusty bolts, my breath was taken away by the sudden freshness of the air. On the side of the turret wall sat the beautiful and serene white gull. A quick glance and then off she went into the kaleidoscope of morning colours.

It was Euan's perception of the gull's sighting that I later found so surprising for he had the mind of a scientist and was not one for fables; he had a logical explanation for everything. The last time I saw the gull was on the tower, that early morning. Euan too saw her, just once more. He had been woken when I rose to follow the footsteps and, not managing to go back to sleep, had taken his labrador out for a walk. The labrador was in and out of the rhododendron bushes, nose to the ground, scuttling about, as labradors do. Euan had been standing on the top bank in front of the house, thinking about Eva. This had been prompted by the recognition of her in a photograph in an old family album, which we had been looking at the previous evening. Without thinking, he called out, 'Eva!' Although spoken softly, the sound of his voice, to himself, seemed to run through the valley. As he stood there the morning sunlight began to spread across the sky and as he looked upwards the white gull came circling round the tower. Three times it circled, finally swooping low, so close that he could have put out his hand and touched it. At last, Euan pondered, Eva had come home to the place that she had cherished and loved. For years afterwards we looked out for this bird but she never did return.

Euan had once told me that Eva had been in love with one of the Macphersons of Balavil, where Allan and Marjorie now lived. Balavil, a vast mansionhouse built in 1770 by Robert Adam, was commissioned by James Ossian Macpherson, who had made his name translating Gaelic poems into English. Balavil has also recently been used as Kilwillie's house in the filming of *Monarch of the Glen* and can be clearly spotted standing up from the A9, just north of Kingussie. During the war this house was utilised as a Commando training centre, after which it lay empty until the mid-sixties, when it was tenanted by Tommy and Jean Macpherson, on a twenty-five year lease. At that time the house was even more noticeable on the journey south, marked as it was by a sentry-box strategically placed at the foot of the drive. Tommy himself was well-known and a prosperous businessman in London. He was also famous for his participation in the Second World War, being the only British soldier to escape from an Italian prisoner-of-war camp.

It was at Balavil, when Tommy and his wife Jean lived there, that we stayed on the infamous night when we were turned out of Glentruim after the reading of the will, and it was also where I acquired my sheltie, Crubie. I had found Balavil cold, yet full of feeling. This house certainly had a ghostly presence and indeed it was well known that a woman had committed suicide over the bridge at the bend of the drive. It was thought that she was a housemaid who had fallen in love with the butler, and with no hope of marriage had killed herself.

The area in which we lived has been Macpherson country for centuries. It is not surprising that there are strange and wonderful tales associated with Macpherson lands and their historical buildings.

# 11

# *The Boy in the Cloth Cap*

THE estate brought in very little income. There were three farms on the Glentruim estate, two of which were tenanted, and eleven other properties which constantly required repairs to be carried out. It was therefore a matter of course that, when our aged retainers retired from their cottages, these cottages should be used for financial gain. When I first proposed this new business of holiday lets to Euan, he was concerned as to what the other landowners would think, but those who had not already pondered the idea were not far behind us in doing so. The old days had passed. Servants were a dying breed and the work generated from an estate like ours often fell heavily on the owners' shoulders. We were no exception: my roles at Glentruim had of necessity to expand to deal with the extra demands of running the estate.

The cottages were basic, three out of the six which we intended to let having their primitive bathroom off the scullery, an arrangement which would certainly not be allowed today. A further four, not intended to let, were at that time left in their original state, without electricity or bathrooms. Lastly, the house at the Home Farm remained as it was, in poor condition but almost habitable.

After gallons of paint were purchased, I was up and down ladders for weeks on end. Some of the centre rugs were left in situ, looking remarkably better with freshly stained surrounds, but there were also rooms that required carpeting. My attempts at tacking down carpets were almost perfect by cottage number six. Having mastered most jobs that were required, there was not much I could not tackle. Making curtains and bedspreads was a struggle. That was because I hated sewing, but gave it my best attempt, and the end results were pleasing. And so, gradually, the cottages were one by one ready for the tourists.

These weathered grey stone cottages that were once the treasured homes of coachmen, gardeners, kennel-boys, ghillies and gamekeepers, and which were bathed in history and memories of the past, then experienced the changing times. The dwellings, now included in holiday photograph-albums, are witness to pleasant holidays for many families. In this modern world, cottages such as these often brought nostalgia to the older visitors and romance to the younger. In the days when they were built, lacking modern machinery, the cumbersome granite boulders would have been brought over from Aberdeen, the Granite City, by horse and cart. No doubt much sweat and toil was put into their construction. These buildings were made to last, and last they did, with their gaping fireplaces and their bulky, dense walls both keeping in the warmth during the winter and letting the heat out in the summer.

Keeper's Cottage and Kennel Cottage overlooked the pond, which during Euan's ancestors' time was used for curling in the winter. Today we still have all types of curling-stones, some being very roughly cast, scattered around the front entrance and the cloakroom. These two cottages stood far enough away to be alone and near enough to be neighbourly, with tall beech trees giving them shelter from the north wind. Twice during the year the honeysuckle creeps up the front of these abodes and stretches below the little windows, trying to find as many nooks and crannies as possible to intrude and grab onto, its soft fragrance enhanced by humidity of the summer days. Newly-cut grass and the scent of pine forests below were an added bonus on such days.

Early in the morning the roe deer come to drink from the pond and wander undisturbed, nibbling the fresh grass in front of the cottage doors from time to time. Surrounded by peace and tranquillity, with only the chirping of birds and the urgent tapping of a distant woodpecker, it is an idyllic place. Just beyond the cottages one can catch a quick glimpse of wide and rich green fields before they slope hurriedly down towards the fast-flowing River Spey, which wends its way gracefully through the valley below. There, the sheep defiantly drift from one field to the other, completely disregarding any rule of fence or dyke. Then, like a shield, the rugged rockface of Craig Dhu soars up behind, a challenge to climbers and a joy to sightseers, impressive and awesome as it looks over all.

I often wondered what stories those buildings could tell. In the days of service, the gamekeeper in his tweed jacket, plus-twos and stalking-hat would stride out at the crack of dawn, with his game-bag on his back, binoculars round his neck, gun half-cocked over one arm and stick in hand. Up over the hills he would go to catch the night predators, such as foxes, buzzards and wild cats before they settled for their customary daytime sleep. Many of these night creatures, however, are protected now. Happy in his solitude, he would observe all that was in his care. There were those great creatures the stags, which proudly carry their heads up high with their antlers spreading above them, and the world-famous grouse, carefully nurtured for the 'Glorious Twelfth' of August when the gamekeeper's skills would be rewarded by the success of the day.

Like the gamekeeper, the ghillie too would rise early to walk the stretches of the river banks. In tweeds and cap, with his waders, bag and rods, he would enjoy the freshness of the riverside as he fished for the larder or culled the scavengers of the waters.

The horses would be snorting and restless in their stable, bursting with energy, impatiently waiting for the stable-boys to finish their chores before the morning ritual of grooming and then exercise. How grand the horse and carriage would have looked by the time they drew up in front of Glentruim's front door.

Meanwhile other workers would be in the walled gardens, busy digging, potting, planting and pruning. Vegetables and flowers would be carefully tended and eventually produced in abundance. There would be enough for all. It was a community all of its own, with everyone working hard in a happy and contented environment, caring and sharing in their families within a family.

In the larger of the two abodes, we were privileged to know Kennedy, the old gardener who had lived at Glentruim since childhood. He was a charming old man, and one could sit and listen all night to his stories, and indeed, we often did. It would be a pleasant little walk after dinner on a summer's evening, with the moon shining down across the pond, the silence broken only by dry twigs and leaves crunching under our feet and by the scuffling of rabbits in the rhododendron bushes. Occasionally we would see a deer darting past, startled by our footsteps, or hear an owl eerily making his presence known.

With bottle in hand, Euan would knock on the door and Kennedy, always eager for company, would touch his forelock and invite us in, our offering gratefully accepted. It was a large place for just one man, and a woman's touch was sadly lacking about the house. A typical Highland croft, it had two bedrooms upstairs, their access being a narrow staircase in the middle with a precarious landing, which lacked banisters, and three rooms downstairs, as well as a pantry and bathroom. Kennedy lived in two of the rooms, which he found to be quite adequate. His bedroom above the warm sitting-room had an old brass bed, a heavy oak dressing-table and a wardrobe. Apart from these essentials the bedroom was bare, whereas the three unused rooms were crammed with furniture and stored belongings. The sitting-room was dimly lit, with an aroma of pipe tobacco, and was kept cosy by the old range fire, which gave out enough heat for the whole house. The evening broth would simmer gently in a big black cast-iron pot hanging high from a hook over the flame in the fire and a mouth-watering smell wafting towards us produced an added quality of homeliness. Amongst the shadows of the room one could see two large armchairs by the fire, which we were always requested to take. A few upright chairs and a table, covered with essential foods and the even more essential bottle of whisky, were the only other furnishings to be seen in this room.

As he sat there glass in hand, with his gentle Highland accent and equally gentle Highland manner, he painted a vivid picture for us of the past, evoking its entire atmosphere. Those happy, carefree and yet hard-working days of childhood, walking miles to the schoolhouse early in the morning and returning in the afternoon just in time for tea. Then there would be kindling to be chopped, peat to be brought in and any other tasks that had been left undone during the day. 'Those were the days,' he would say repeatedly, and one could not help feeling the wish to have lived in 'those days' also.

Having reminisced and put the world to rights, we would reluctantly leave the glow of the fire and head for home. Kennedy would don his cap and with stick in hand would accompany us to the top of the path, then raise his cap as we parted to bid us goodnight.

It was a very sad day when Kennedy became too old and ill to live alone and had to leave the place to be looked after by his sister. Yet another era was gone, to be committed to memory alone. He left a few things behind, including the old brass bed. It seemed fitting that it should stay where it belonged and where no doubt his whole family had enjoyed their days. So I left this brass bed in the main bedroom, ready for holiday lets.

The sky was blue, it was hot, and summer was at its best the day

90

the first party from the south arrived to collect the cottage keys. In all there were six of them and they had taken both the Keeper's Cottage and the Kennel Cottage. Bright young teachers not long out of college, and some of them already in their first jobs. They were happy and excited at the prospect of their holiday. Having had a long journey, I thought that a cup of tea would be refreshing for them, so invited them into the drawing-room. They were glancing around at the family portraits on the walls as we talked about Euan's family and the clan of which he was a chieftain. I then showed them the small museum in the room next door, which contained so much of the Macpherson history.

Eventually we sat down to refreshments and the inevitable question arose.

'Is there a ghost?'

Knowing that some people have a genuine fear of the thought of seeing a ghost, I gave the answer as evasively as possible, especially since they were staying in two of the properties.

After tea, I took them up to the cottages and showed them around what were to be their homes for the following two weeks. They looked neat and tidy, a smell of fresh paint still lingering on. An open fire was a great treat for them, and one of the young men immediately put a match to the bundle of kindling in the Keeper's Cottage, which had been carefully arranged in the hearth. The girls were delighted with the newly-picked flowers in vases on the tables and even more pleased to see pretty matching curtains and bedspreads in the bedrooms. It gave me great pleasure to see my hard work appreciated, and I hoped that they would be the first of many satisfied customers.

The surroundings of the cottages were a dream on such a day. The pond was clear, the birds were singing and my peacocks walked around the edge of the pond, pecking out their lunch from the grass that had been newly cut that morning. The oldest peacock guardedly fanned his tail as the others eyed the newcomers with suspicion and perhaps also wondered whether any food scraps could be expected!

At the beginning of the second week we were asked up for an apéritif in Keeper's Cottage. I presumed that our visitors wished to reciprocate my hospitality, but soon found out that there was a little more to it than that.

It was early evening when we walked along the path and I was reminded very much of the last time we had walked to be entertained in Keeper's Cottage, when visiting that kind old man, and of the tales of the long past which I learnt from him. I entered with mixed feelings. We were given a hearty welcome, for our guests were obviously enjoying themselves and were in high spirits. As I took the glass of wine offered to me I remembered the whisky, and as a dining-room chair was drawn to me, I remembered the old armchair. But there was no black pot over the fire, no pipe-smoke and no gentle Highland voice. No story tonight I thought, but I was wrong.

We heard much about their careers and families, and everyone was relaxed. They asked Euan numerous questions about his family, about the estate and once more the old favourite, but this time it was a little different: they asked if Keeper's Cottage was haunted. To our knowledge, at that time, our answer was, 'No'. We related at length the history of the cottage and of its occupants. Then, as we all sat around the fire with our glasses of wine, there was silence in the room before the tale began.

The Hazelwoods, who had booked the cottages, had the first choice of bedroom in Keeper's Cottage and their preference was Kennedy's room. Four of them were in this cottage and two in the other. They had walked into the room above the sitting-room and just loved it, the charming décor and the old brass bed, in addition to which was the outlook over the pond and the birch wood with the hills in the distance. 'What peace – a dream,' they enthused. For them it was a rarity to see roe deer in the early morning and evening, numerous birds and also my peacocks. The scene was described as being magical.

On the first night the Hazelwoods did not sleep well. They had found themselves listening for every sound. They heard the deer walking by, the occasional owl and every creak and groan imaginable in the cottage. The next day was busy and they felt sure that sleep would come easily. Normally, we told them because Glentruim is at an altitude of over 1,000 feet, most of our house-visitors slept like logs.

They continued with their story. It was a fairly early night for all and they did sleep soundly until about two o'clock in the morning. They woke to the discomfort of the bed being shaken, and neither had been awake long before the movement abruptly stopped. The wife then spoke slowly as she watched the flames leap in the hearth. She told us that, while looking around the moonlit room, all looked as before with the exception of the large shadow of the bed greedily occupying the whole of one wall. All was quiet, she had said, not even a creature of the night seemed to stir.

Then it was her husband's turn to speak, his eyes wide as he watched our reactions carefully, as if willing us to believe all he was about to tell. A couple of nights later, having almost totally dismissed the idea of anything strange ever happening, he had fallen into a sound sleep. It had been sultry yet clear, and the window had been wide open, as had the curtains. Before falling asleep, he had thought how still everything was and how unnerving the silence could be if you were not used to it. They were accustomed to the bustle of a town, with continual noise of some sort going on. Cars, voices, aeroplanes, footsteps on pavements and dogs barking were their familiar sounds of the night. Not long after he had fallen asleep the feeling of being jostled began again. Awaking immediately, he had sat bolt upright in bed and the movement slowly stopped. He recalled a pronounced chill throughout the room and a strange feeling that ran up and down his back. We all sat there almost holding our breaths as he continued. He had sat up in bed and remained motionless and uncomfortably rigid. A strong awareness of unknown company had compelled him to stare across the room. His eyes, as if guided, had been drawn towards the door and, there, standing quite still and returning his glance, was a young boy in a cloth cap. The boy was simply dressed in a brown jacket and knee-length trousers. There was a scarf around his neck and he looked as if he had been working, ruffled and tired. The storyteller paused for a few seconds before informing us that the apparition was gone as quickly as it had come. I had noted the pallor on his face and dryness of his mouth as he narrated this tale and, by the expression on the faces of his friends, he had obviously not told the others of his experience until this night.

The apparition appeared once more, this time to both husband and wife. Euan and I were intrigued by the whole affair and I said to them that perhaps the old man who had previously lived in the cottage must have died, unbeknown to us, and returned here as a boy. I could hear him saying so clearly, 'Those were the days.' Perhaps he had gone back to those 'good old days', the days he had loved so dearly and when he had been so content.

A few weeks later, I learnt from the obituary column in the local paper that Kennedy had died. Clearly he had still been alive at the time of the sighting of the 'boy in the cloth cap', but perhaps just before his death his last memories had taken his spirit back to his place of childhood. Who knows?

# 12

# *At Home*

I very much enjoyed having Euan's sister, Marie, to stay; she like Euan, spent much of her youth at Glentruim. During her holidays with us there would undoubtedly be a drama of some sort or another! I recall the day when she and I were on our way out to lunch and while driving down the avenue I said to Marie that we would stop briefly at the Lodge, which was situated at the foot of the drive. It had to be checked prior to holiday visitors coming to stay there the next day. Passing what we called Pelham's Drive, which was a dirt track going up into the woods, I told Marie of a strange occurrence that I had experienced with Catriona. It had happened on the way back from school one afternoon just before Pelham's Drive. Both Catriona and I had seen a man standing in our way, who then darted up the rough unmade road just as we were approaching him. 'Watch where he goes,' I said to Catriona, as I turned into the track and followed him. We had been troubled with poachers and I suspected that this would be one of them. We stopped at a tall, thick, old oak tree, behind which the figure had disappeared. I jumped out of the Land Rover to search behind the tree but there was nobody there and nowhere that he could have run to without me noticing. I asked Catriona to describe this apparition. 'It was a man in a long, dark cloak, with a hood over his head.' Catriona described him perfectly, exactly as I too had observed him. When I told Euan what had taken place, he informed me that this particular oak tree used to be where sheep poachers were hanged! There was no explanation for what we had seen. Naturally, I had wondered whether this could have been the ghost of the hangman. However, I later heard from Joan Richardson, our doctor's wife, that although the main gibbet had formerly been over at the crooked bridge on the Glentruim back road, this instrument of ultimate punishment was later moved to the Catlodge area, beyond Glentruim. The change was made, Joan told me, for the simple reason that from the dining-room at the castle, Cluny's wife objected to seeing bodies swinging in the wind as she sat at breakfast.

'My goodness,' Marie had said, after she heard about the incident that I had experienced with Catriona, 'What strange things happen at Glentruim!' I pulled up in front of the Lodge door, and told Marie that I would not be long. I first went into the bedroom on the left of the front door, where the curtains were closed and the temperature in the room felt very warm. I had not remembered shutting the curtains and I was sure that I had not turned on the heating. As I bent down to switch on the bedside light, within the little streak of light that shone between the window-drapes, my eyes met another person's staring back at me! There was a man in the bed! I automatically let out a muffled scream before leaving the room. 'There's a man in the bed,' I exclaimed to Marie, who was sitting patiently in the Land Rover. 'No!' her voice portrayed her horror. Doubting myself, I re-entered and by this time the man was hastily pulling on his trousers, tripping as he did so.

'What do you think you are doing here?' I demanded, furious that this dirty young man should be lying in my clean sheets. The thought of having to re-make the bed was far more of a nuisance to me than the presence of a vagrant! Without waiting for an answer, I asked, 'And how did you get in?'

'I came in for shelter out of the storm,' he replied, 'The door had been blown open by the wind.'

He then told me that he had fallen off his motorbike along the back road, and had left his vehicle in a ditch. I told him to hurry up and finish getting dressed and then I would take him to his motorbike. Whether I was shaking because of my irritation or because of the fright he had given me I did not know. Probably both.

The young man got into the back of the Land Rover and I watched him carefully in the front windscreen mirror. As he sat down he asked me for a cigarette but I told him that we had none. I then looked more carefully at his reflection in the mirror and, noticing a distinctly vacant look about his face, I became increasingly nervous. Not far along the road I asked him to get out of the car and then drove straight home to contact the police.

The police picked him up and later telephoned me to say how stupid I had been. There was no motorbike and this young fellow had been high on drugs. 'You could have had your throat slit,' said the police officer. 'He had a knife in his pocket!' I felt ashamed that I had put Marie and indeed myself in danger, but I was still very cross about having to change the sheets. I told Marie of our lucky escape, to which she replied, 'Yes indeed, another strange happening at Glentruim!'

We did go to our lunch date, arriving rather late, but on our return we checked the cottage once more and found that a back window had been broken. That was yet another problem to be dealt with before our holiday visitors arrived!

Marie and I were continually trying to think of another business to provide finance for the upkeep of Glentruim. We even started making baby haggis, which we called hagglets. We travelled up to the slaughterhouse in Granton-on-Spey to fetch lengths of sheep's colon, which we then washed and hung to dry over all of the cupboard handles in the kitchen. This was in preparation for filling them with our different haggis recipes. Cauldrons full of offal, other ingredients and different liqueurs would be boiling away for hours on top of the old range and electric cooker. We sent samples to different companies and awaited their opinion. The idea was to rent a room in the factory down by the railway station in Newtonmore, and to churn out our selection of hagglets. This product was then to be packaged in little boxes, tied with tartan ribbon. One large well-known chain store was interested, but I gave up the idea when I contemplated the rigorous rules and regulations surrounding the food industry. We did have fun, though, with this project, especially when we saw the expression on friends' faces when they looked at what was hanging around the kitchen!

Angie Bain, the retired keeper from Glenbanchor, came to work for us whenever he could, his many years of experience benefiting us all at Glentruim. He would accompany Euan on the hill and also take shooting guests out for the day. I did not actually know Angie's wife, Anne, very well until much later, after Angie had died. Anne and I then became close friends, indeed she was like a granny to our children. She knew every proverb to be known and would have a saying for every happening or circumstance you could imagine. Her words of wisdom were a volume of knowledge for our children, and they learnt a great deal from her, as did I. We cleaned many a cottage together, she helped me with innumerable tasks and we confided our thoughts and feelings to each other over the years.

Anne and her friend, Isobel Carr, enjoyed coming to assist me with functions, and it was often during the drinks we had together after each party that we had the most laughs. We would sit around the kitchen table, glasses filled, talking about the events of the day and reminiscing. I remember these conversations fondly.

'I will never forget one weekend when you were all away and Isobel and I stayed at Glentruim. Were we glad to get back home to our own beds! I don't think either of us slept a bit,' Anne said once.

'That's right,' Isobel chipped in. 'I had heard in the village that there was the ghost of a butler that haunted Glentruim and I was sure that he would appear. Then, on that first night, it must have been in the early hours of the morning, we heard the sound of sawing, which we thought was coming from the basement. Do you remember that Anne?'

'Could I forget? And the peacocks were scratching on the roof and the flag-pole was rattling.'

Isobel took over again: 'Then around 4 a.m. we heard this loud bang! Both of us were terrified, but we went out bravely into the corridor, in our nighties, to investigate. It was those two long, Indian rifles, inlaid with mother-of-pearl, which had been precariously propped up against the wall, on top of the central heating cover. They must have gradually shifted, hence the sawing noise, and then they had clattered down!'

'It was the vibration of the central heating coming on,' Anne added, 'but I think we had scared each other that night: too many ghost stories before we went to bed!'

I recalled a similar situation during my first few months at Glentruim when my friend Vicky was staying. We were alone in the house, sitting in the smoking-room, which was the only fully furnished room at the time. Feeling 'spooked' by the house, we sat huddled in front of a healthy fire, almost expecting something to happen. Then there was a loud thud from the hall. Both of us, with hearts pounding, went out into the somewhat sinister hall where the stags' heads looked down on us, adding to our unrest. We noticed that the grandfather clock had stopped at the same moment that we had heard the thud. The pendulum of the grandfather clock had fallen down to the bottom of its case!

'Do you remember your daffodil party?' Isobel asked. 'We had a fair good drink that night, champagne, if I recall, and Mrs Macpherson had given me a bag of goodies to take home, which her labrador ate while we were all gossiping.'

'Well, at least the dog wasn't having stillborn puppies under the kitchen table as we prepared the food, like the spaniel, the time of that afternoon tea-party – Vicky was here too!' Anne reminded us, and we all giggled.

Everyone who was invited to the daffodil party was asked to dress in yellow. It was held on the lawns in front of Glentruim, which were fringed with thousands of colourful daffodils of all varieties. Inside the house, more daffodils had been arranged in every container possible and were placed everywhere. Even the food prepared was yellow to match the daffodils.

One function which Anne recollected was the champagne breakfast that we held for the Salmon Smokers Association. I had made all of the dishes with smoked salmon, including a sorbet! 'The Campbell girls, Ann and Isobel, helped serve at table that day and John MacIntosh, who lives down the road from me, played the pipes,' Anne added.

Euan would be the perfect host when we entertained and would be eager to recount the history of the clan and his family in great detail. His life was devoted to Glentruim, and it was apparent when he talked so proudly about his heritage.

Our holidays, however, were few; what we loved most was having our friends to stay. Bill Ayles, Euan's close friend since student days, who was also the best man at our wedding, would come to Glentruim for weekends with his wife, Mary. Looking back to my first meeting with the Ayles family, when we lived in Edinburgh, I remember thinking that I was not much older than Bill and Mary's children. This never proved to be a problem for Bill and Mary, who accepted me as I was, but I did encounter difficulties with some of Euan's other friends' wives. I suspect that they thought I was too young and immature for Euan, and perhaps posed a threat, their husbands being so attentive towards me. I was certainly relieved when we moved to the Highlands, where all ages mixed together very comfortably.

Glentruim represented a natural playground for our children, and they often had their own playmates to stay. They would be out in the garden all day, given fine summer weather, only coming inside for meals and to go to sleep. Some youngsters were not totally at ease in the house, especially when Catriona and Lachlan gave them a tour of the gloomy, unlit dungeons. By the time they went to bed, their imaginations were running wild! The other element in the house, which could bother both children and adults, was the colony of bats that lived in the attic space. These bats would swoop down the corridors at great speed, making those unfortunate enough to be walking there duck or retreat to the nearest room. Sleeping bats hung on curtains and during the night they would even come in through an open window or down a chimney. Catriona once said to me, 'My school friends think we are like the Adams Family!'

Sadly, Euan frequently despaired about the viability of the estate, and we would sit for hours in the evening wondering whether we would ever be able to carry on there. There were countless nights when we talked about selling, but in the morning, when we looked out across the valley, so beautiful and still, or wandered through the home that we had made for ourselves, all amalgamated with the past, we soon changed our minds. Moving forward stalwartly, Euan carried on as usual with his job in Inverness and then toiled for hours on the estate during each weekend, just as I too ploughed all my energy into keeping Glentruim.

# 13

# *Halfway House*

HALFWAY House lies totally out of sight of any other dwelling, and is well-named, being halfway between Laggan and Dalwhinnie, off the old road originally built by General Wade. Its nearest neighbour is Catlodge, situated at the west end of the Glentruim back road, and in this vicinity is a memorial cairn built to the memory of Calum Piobair. The ancient traditions of serious bagpipers owes much to this family of Macpherson pipers, whose teachings were directly passed down the generations, their musical knowledge and skills originating from the MacCrimmons of Skye.

John MacDonald, probably the most distinguished pupil of Calum Piobair, was born in 1865 at Glentruim, the son of Sandy MacDonald, gamekeeper and ground officer to Colonel Macpherson of Glentruim. Latterly known as John MacDonald of Inverness, he was brought up in the glen. In due course his pupils handed down the MacCrimmon music to the present day.

We have a very clear old photograph of Calum Piobair standing in Highland dress, his beard long and white, holding a stout, knotted stick. Also in our possession is a very old set of bagpipes made by Duncan MacDougall of Aberfeldy. Interestingly the chanter, which must have been replaced, was made by William Ross, piper to Queen Victoria. These, at one time in permanent use, are still treasured today; I can only assume they were played by Glentruim pipers or by members of the family.

The best view of Halfway House is seen as you travel south from Catlodge, wending your way up through the hills. There it is, straight from a picture postcard, this isolated little white-washed cottage. It is situated at the side of the road, with a green painted door and a window on either side. Both windows have shutters, which are securely bolted when the house is un-occupied. Over a fence from the small surrounding garden stretches miles of empty moorland, thick with gorse and heather, hills rambling up and over as far as the main road. On the Laggan side of the cottage is a small bridge over a stream, which follows the road down from the hill, after passing a small wood of Scots pine. When we came to live at Glentruim, Halfway House lay empty for most of the year, only being used as a lunchtime stop during days of shooting on the hill. It was always a prime target for breaking and entering.

Before Euan inherited Glentruim, we had a taste of the primitive life when we stayed in Halfway House for long week-ends. It was a typical but and ben, with two main rooms down-stairs and a little scullery behind the staircase, then two bedrooms upstairs divided by a narrow landing. All the walls downstairs were tongue-and-grooved, painted white, and there were wood-stained floors scarcely covered with the odd tattered rug. The room on the left of the front door had two comfortable arm-chairs, a roughly-made wooden bookcase, an old but serviceable couch and coffee-tables dotted around. The room to the right served as an eating area, with a sizeable square dining-table which could be extended, six upright chairs and a dark oak corner-cabinet full of old china. Light entered the two upstairs rooms by skylights in the low coom ceiling. These two rooms were furnished with the bare essentials of two single beds divided by a small bedside table and a single wooden chair, both rooms being mirror images of each other.

There was no electricity in Halfway House, which added to the mystery of the place, particularly when the paraffin lamps and candles were lit each night. There was a rusty old butane-gas cooker in the scullery and a deep sink, which only had one tap with cold running water from the stream. Euan had plumbed in the water himself and these pipes gave constant trouble, blocking or freezing in the winter. Most of the cooking was carried out in black pots or on the spit over the open fireplaces, which were merely large holes in the walls of the downstairs rooms. A chemical toilet, situated in a rugged lean-to, was a later addition to the house, but, when the midges were about, you had to be quick! I remember once, having made a visit, totally covered from head to foot, including a balaclava on my head, coming back in and being left with a mask-like patch of bites on my face – the midges never missed an opportunity.

While we were still living in Edinburgh, Halfway House was well within reach to spend the night after social evenings such as the Annual Regimental Ball of the Scottish Horse, a detachment raised by the dukes of Atholl, held at Blair Atholl Castle. One year, when we had mustered a party of eight, six of us carried on up to Halfway House for a long weekend. Among those who came with us were two colleagues of Euan's, as well as Archie Walls and Sally Nugent. I had known Archie for years. Indeed, after our wedding, he had drawn a very clever sketch of Euan and myself standing by our wedding cake as a thank-you card. My friendship with Sally went back many years, because we had been at school together, rode our horses together, then finally trained as nurses at the same hospital.

We arrived at Halfway House in the early hours of the morning, only to find campers had pitched their tent in the front garden. Opening the gate and parking our cars behind the house did not seem to rouse them. Wickedly, as quiet as church mice, we undid the padlock on the front door, turned the large key in the lock, and then without a sound, unbolted the shutters from the inside of the window, placing them against the outside walls of the building. Our men were in full Highland dress and we ladies in ballgowns and tartan sashes. We formed a circle and, with only six people, danced the Eightsome Reel, shouting and singing at the top of our voices. Three heads appeared from the tent, and before they were fully awake, the campers dismantled their tent and were off, as we continued our prankish conduct.

Later that morning the men went over the hill to hunt for our supper and duly brought back a roe in the late afternoon. Once the animal had been prepared and was hanging on the spit over the fire, cooking gently, we exchanged stories, enjoying heat from the fire and paraffin lamps, and inner warmth from the whisky while the aroma of venison teased our tastebuds.

The blackcock, a game bird, was prominent in this area. It has become rare over recent years and, for the majority of people, can only be seen in places such as Kingussie Wildlife Park. It must be one of the most exciting experiences that I have ever had to watch the 'lek' at Halfway House. During the mating season of these birds, with precise timing, you can watch the lek, which is when the male birds choose their females.

In 1971, not long after Sally married, she and her husband Donald Crystal (owner of Tombuie Smoke House near Aberfeldy) came to stay with us for a weekend at Halfway House. Donald woke us all up at 4 a.m. and we went outside together in our night attire to watch the lek. One by one the blackcock appeared, dropping from their roosts, and formed a circle, thirty-six of them in all. It was a dramatic spectacle. Fanning their tails, showing off their distinctive black and white feathers, the males danced round and round to their audience of females. One is lucky to see this once in a lifetime, but Euan and I frequently made the effort to get up to watch this incredible sight, which we caught on so many early mornings. Those were happy and carefree days.

There was one book in the corner cupboard of the dining-room in Halfway House, covered in mildew and entitled *Happy Hawkers*. This was written by Elizabeth Macpherson and published in 1937. Latterly, she and her husband, Ian, had spent their happiest days at Halfway House. I cherished this book and repeatedly read it from cover to cover during the long evenings by the fire while staying in Halfway House. What made it even more special to me was that Elizabeth had inscribed her signature on the first page. They were both teachers from Aberdeen, with one thing in common – they hated teaching. Giving up everything, they took to the road, as hawkers, initially buying and selling china from their old car. Building up their business, they carried on hawking, with no licence to do so, later branching out into vegetables and fruit. Their customers were the people of Badenoch and Strathspey. As their trade expanded they acquired a trailer and a caravan to live in, which was kept in the valley. They mixed with the locals and became well-known for their fresh produce and also for their stories, which they picked up from village to village. They were particularly fond of the Dalwhinnie and one day, while in this area, stumbled on Halfway House. Finding the door locked but coming across an unsnibbed window at the back, they crept in and fell in love with the place. They found out that it belonged to the Glentruim estate and subsequently rented it for a year for the princely sum of one pound a month.

Like those perplexed campers on the night of the Blair Atholl Ball, they too had their stories to tell. They wrote of a ghost-house nine miles beyond Benalder Lodge and fifteen miles from Dalwhinnie, near the west end of Loch Ericht. This dwelling was built behind the desolation of Rannoch Moor, an empty place avoided by the locals of that time. It was said that the place was haunted by a woman who had taken refuge there from the storms. With her was her child and, as the story goes, being crazed by hunger, she killed and then ate her child! Elizabeth and Ian never did hawk their wares in that vicinity.

Being hidden away, Halfway House was frequently broken into. Usually nothing was taken or damaged inside; the house was mainly entered for shelter, by those who tried to exert squatters' rights. I would religiously check Halfway House at least once a week, and it was not unusual to have to deal with intruders. They nearly always gained access through the same window as Ian and Elizabeth Macpherson, but, unlike the Macphersons, they would either break the lock, the window, or both.

After one of the regular break-ins, having yet again come across squatters, I let their car tyres down, before driving home to contact the police. On the telephone to the police officer, I told him that he need not hurry and confessed what I had done. In reply I was told, 'I did not hear that Madam – that is an offence, don't mention it when my colleague arrives!' Meeting back at Halfway House, I was amused to hear the police officer tell the young foreigners that there was no such thing as squatters' rights in Scotland! To their embarrassment they were made to go out the way they came in.

The end of the Glentruim back road, where it meets the Dalwhinnie–Laggan road, was where the children were picked up by the school car. Quite often in good weather, when we had plenty of time, we would make this journey on ponies, through the fields along the banks of the Spey. Catriona soon learned to ride and would be on her own pony, but Lachlan, being so much younger, would sit in front of me on mine. All of us rode bareback, a fairly easy ride on the Garrons, which were broad, hardy ponies. We kept them in the fields above the policies and had an arrangement of barter: we gave grazing to Cameron Ormiston for his trekking ponies in exchange for the enjoyment of riding them.

It was a Friday. I knew I should make a visit to Halfway House, not having managed to go earlier in the week, but on this particular hot summer's afternoon I had decided to pick up the children on horseback. I favoured a challenging ride for, having had my own horses throughout my life until I was married, I missed the excitement of showjumping, dressage and cross-country events. My twin sister and I had been members of the Perth Pony Club when we were young and would travel miles with our horses for Three Day Events. The Garron I rode over Glentruim was high-spirited and a good ride but did not compare with some of the fine horses I used to have. When riding to meet the school car, I would get to my destination far more quickly than on the ride back, when I had Catriona's pony on a long lungeing-rein. How refreshing it was to be out enjoying the countryside! The Garrons were sure-footed ponies and able to tackle all bogs, gorse and heather. This was one of the reasons for using this particular breed of pony to bring the deer down from the hill during stalking, the other being their immense strength. Their distinctive smell added pleasure to my ride, reminding me of those numerous days of mucking out, grooming and loading horses into horseboxes ready for the journey to the various horse-shows.

Having returned home on the day that I had collected the children on horseback, the ponies were back in their field and the children, after tea, were reluctantly doing their homework. The telephone rang and it was the local police. 'Sorry to bother you Ma'am, but I will tell you what it is,' said the officer. 'Halfway House belongs to you, doesn't it?' With my confirmation, he continued, 'Well I hate to tell you this – I have something terrible to tell you.' I was prepared to be told about another break-in, so there was no surprise in my voice when I asked him what it was. 'When patrolling the area, we noticed that the front door of Halfway House had been tampered with, the padlock was off and the lock broken.' More expense, I thought; these people would be charged, but they never paid for the damage. 'There's more,' he stated, on a more sombre note, 'I am afraid that what we found was shocking. On entering we found a tramp who was hanging on a rope from the landing banisters. Dead of course, Ma'am.' Having heard this, I realised how fortunate I had been that afternoon. The summer's day had saved me from a visit to Halfway House. It would have been bad enough for me to see that sight, but for the children it would have been horrifying.

Later, I told Catriona about the incident; she looked perplexed, then started to tell me about the previous Saturday. I had gone out shopping and, it being such a lovely sunny day, Euan had decided to cut the grass while the children played outside. At some stage in the afternoon, when Catriona was outside dealing with the guinea-pigs, a tramp appeared in the garden. He was tall with a shaven head, dirty and wore a long beige coat which almost touched his old string-laced boots. He was hungry Catriona had said, so she had given him some apples from the orchard. She then told him that he had better go, before her father saw him! He did as he was told and obediently walked back down the drive with his apples. Catriona, being frightened by his visit, had run across the lawn and down the banks, looking for her father. She did not plan to tell her father about the tramp in case he was cross. The description of the tramp who took his life at Halfway House fitted that of the person Catriona had met that sunny day.

The next strange coincidence was when Ian Richardson, our local doctor, came to visit the following weekend. He told us that he had picked up a tramp walking up the back road between Halfway House and Dalwhinnie. Ian had asked him where he was destined for, to which the reply was Edinburgh. Because of the state that this poor fellow was in, Ian suggested that he took him home for a meal and a wash. However, his kind offer was turned down and the tramp asked to get out of the car. From his front mirror Ian could see the tramp walk stealthily back to where he had being staying – Halfway House.

So there was both happiness and sadness in Halfway House. There was joy for Ian and Elizabeth and all those who rested there, and then, sadly, it was the place chosen by the tramp to end his life.

To a certain extent, Halfway House saw the introduction of

nutrition into the valley. I could imagine how gratifying it must have been for the local doctors when Ian and Elizabeth arrived with their fresh fruit and vegetables, thus helping to contribute to the reduction of scurvy in the Highlands. When we arrived in Glentruim it was hard to find the fresh vegetables that we had been used to being able to buy in the city of Edinburgh. Mostly there were only root vegetables and even the fruit was basic. Avocado pears were unheard of, but a pear from pear trees was well-kent and would be offered instead.

All was not lost in Strathspey and Badenoch as far as market-produce was concerned after Ian and Elizabeth had left; fruit and vegetable shops were soon established. Also, in April 1970 the Nield brothers introduced the more exotic fresh fruit and vegetables in their shop in Kingussie, which was called Murchie's. This was a revelation to us all, and once again I could buy the variety of produce which I had been so accustomed to in the city. The shop was also a delicatessen and, if a particular item was requested which was not in stock, it would be ordered immediately and thereafter stacked on their shelves.

Freddy and Bobby Nield claimed to be descended from the Vikings, and they came first into the valley during the construction of the new road to the Highlands. They both drove lorries, bringing the necessary requirements for this road, which was to bypass so many of the little villages and became one of the most dangerous roads in Scotland. The reason for its hazardous condition, I believe, was that it continually changed from dual carriageway to single road and, furthermore, some of the on-coming lanes of dual carriageway were obscured from each other.

Glentruim had the advantage of having a large walled garden on the north side, which was well placed in a hollow and captured sun all day long. Unfortunately, our young gardener could not keep on top of the weeds and cultivate vegetables. The gooseberry, blackcurrant and raspberry bushes had taken over, along with the overgrown and intrusive rhubarb. I tried my hand at planting rows of winter vegetables, only to be beaten by the rabbits and the deer. This walled garden was badly in need of repair and was useless without well-maintained masonry and deer- and rabbit-proof fencing. After back-breaking efforts I gave up and concentrated on the rose bushes at the top of the garden, which lay in front of a lean-to greenhouse at the back wall. In this greenhouse I cultivated pot-plants for the house and brought on seedlings for the house garden. Above the greenhouse stood a bower of honeysuckle, beneath which a seat had been constructed by Euan's ancestors, rather too close to eight bee-hives, certainly too close for my liking. When the honeysuckle blossomed it was a source of nectar for the busy resident bees. At the other side of the far wall there was an ornate summer-house which must have been a romantic place in more leisurely days. It had been put together with lengths of birch and family names had been endearingly carved into the wood. Also, behind this summer house was a very large shed which housed an old generator, no longer in use – a most dangerous place for children. The generator had been dropped into a vast open hole. There were so many hidden places on Glentruim, a haven for formerly hide-and-seek nooks and crannies, formerly complemented by a well-stocked garden of vegetables and fruit for all who resided there.

# 14

# *The Local Medical Practice*

IAN Richardson, our local doctor, was one of those characters that all Highland villages should have. He was well-respected, someone to look up to, highly intelligent, full of mirth and had boundless stories to tell. Ian and his wife Joan came from Edinburgh, where they had lived in a large house surrounded by a council estate. Having tolerated vast quantities of rubbish thrown into their garden and graffiti on their boundary walls, they decided to look for a practice in the country, preferably the Highlands of Scotland. They had six children in all and having been offered the Laggan practice, they moved into the Doctor's House. Both Ian and Joan supported the village activities and were immediately accepted by the locals. They became 'pillars of the community'.

Ian, being the local doctor, was the first person we came to know when we arrived north, because of my pregnancy. He soon became my confidant, friend, adviser and even my first plumber! Our initial winter was bitterly cold, and cold houses are prone to frozen pipes. Late one evening, when alone in the house, I heard an ominous drip coming from the smoking-room and, following investigation, found water coming through the ceiling above one of the windows. Knowing no plumber at that time, I phoned Ian. By the time he arrived the drip had developed into a steady stream and I feared that the ceiling might collapse. Ian rolled up his sleeves and got to work on a frozen pipe in the bathroom above the smoking-room. He had had plenty of practice. Soon all was fixed and I was given the name and telephone number of a local plumber for the future.

No visit from Ian was complete without a story or two by the fire. When Euan was at home the whisky bottle would come out for the evening. Euan would have a dram while Ian, who never drank alcohol, pretended to – then tales would unfold. We both enjoyed Ian's company immensely: he was a brilliantly clever man and could make the gloomiest of stories sound hysterical. A born entertainer, as he sat down we knew we were in for a long evening of hilarity. His stories were told behind a stretched hand, head turned to the side, in a gesture of secrecy, a mannerism characteristic of Ian, during which his eyes lit up in devilment and a chuckle was sure to follow.

Ian liked deer-stalking as much as Euan, and even though he rented shooting over Benalder he was also always welcome on Glentruim, where he and Euan dragged many a beast down from the hill together. Ian frequently had a rifle in the back of his car in case he came across a deer on his travels through Glentruim or Benalder. He told us one evening how one of the locals had been coming home over the moor, shot a stag and dragged it into the boot of his car, only to discover, halfway home, that it was still alive. All Ian's unique stories, such as this, were soon stored in our memory banks just as they had been in his.

Not many days went by when a doctor was not called out to an accident on the busy main road and Ian therefore often had to deal with victims of severe car crashes. Because of the frequency of these incidents, Ian was one of the instigators of the helicopter service which uplifted casualties and took them to Raigmore Hospital in Inverness. He was also known for his skill with hypnosis, which he was frequently asked to use.

Ian was good to us and would make house calls, rather than ask us to wait in his surgery, whenever it was at all possible. A true emergency visit was once required when Euan's mother had been staying and Euan, in the course of taking the combs of honey from the beehives, got stung by hundreds of bees. Peter MacDonald, our ghillie, also an expert in beekeeping, had been gradually teaching Euan how to look after bees. Both Peter and his wife, whom the children called Doggal, were so good to us during our early years at Glentruim. Doggal was always ready to help me when I was busy and often looked after the children for us. On the day Peter and Euan were dealing with the bees Euan had accidentally let the top of a hive slip and the sudden movement had caused angry bees to swarm all over him. He ran up from the garden, at the same time wringing out his bee-covered shirt. I was in the conservatory with Euan's mother and Catriona, but seeing him totally covered in bees, with not one inch left uncovered, I asked his mother quickly to take the pram and baby down the drive. Euan thrashed away at the bees until most had gone away and then he lay in shock on the smoking-room couch. I had already called the doctor, but realised the extreme urgency when I saw his throat swelling as he gasped for breath. I knew that the snake-bite kit in the hall drawer would have helped, since it contained an ampoule of adrenaline and cortisone, but, when I checked, it was out-of-date. Euan's condition was deteriorating and I knew that I might have to carry out a tracheotomy. I was beginning to panic as I looked for a sharp knife with a thin tip. Thankfully Ian arrived just as I was poised and ready to do what had to be done, which filled me with terror, and he gave Euan the antidote. Soon he began to recover and Ian felt that it was safe to leave. Thereafter Euan was very cautious when working with the bees, so much so, I remember him once putting on his diving gear, mask and all, before he went to retrieve the honey!

After the bee incident, a discussion with Ian regarding the out-of-date ampoules in the snake-bite kit led us to talk about how many times Euan had been bitten by adders. Indeed Ian had written about this for the *British Medical Journal*. To date he had

114

been bitten three times, and according to the *BMJ* this was a record. Usually the snakes struck Euan's legs, when he was wearing the kilt. The first was when our whole family had gone up to check the water-tank on the hill, which involved a long walk up with thick ferns and heather underfoot. Euan had opened the stiff door at the top end of the tank and the noise had disturbed an adder, which immediately bit him on the arm. It was a hasty walk home to call for Ian to come and give him the antidote. The adder bites that followed were all on Euan's legs and occurred when he was up shooting on the hill, burning heather or scything long grass in the policies. One could understand why Ian had given me the antidote kit to keep at home!

My ailments were few and I was so busy that I would prefer treatments to be carried out in the surgery rather than the hospital, if possible. It was for this reason that I asked Ian to remove two moles, which looked to me as if they could become troublesome. I was told to go to the doctor's house at surgery closing-time. To begin with, Ian, Joan and I sat in their sitting-room having a good old gossip, with refreshments to cheer us on, and then it was time for the minor surgery. On to the table I went with Ian assisted by Joan. Remarks such as, 'Oh dear, it is deeper than I thought', and, 'Maybe I should have referred you', in between the odd bout of laughter made me have second thoughts. Too late! Afterwards I drove myself home in the Land Rover, but as the local anaesthetic wore off, one of the incisions, close to the hard seat on which I sat, began to throb. The one under my arm took longer to cause pain, but the analgesics I had been given did nothing for the discomfort I was to experience that night.

There was one unusual phenomenon concerning myself which Ian enthusiastically described for a medical journal. I had driven up to Inverness to collect my sister and her new baby at the airport. By the time we arrived home I had produced milk for her baby. I could not believe this had happened, but thought it was probably because Zoë and I were twins. When I told Ian, he said that this was quite common in primitive countries and that when the baby left, the milk would go too. He was right and I was mistaken about the precipitating factor of being a twin of the baby's mother. I later discovered this when visiting a friend recently home from hospital with her baby!

When Ian retired it was a sad day for the community. The old-fashioned country doctor with the gentle bedside manner was part of a dying race and almost nonexistent in towns. My father had also been a GP in the village of Stanley, in Perthshire, and when I was a child I used to sit in his car while he visited his patients. I always knew there would be a long wait and could imagine him sitting on the side of the bed, being a good listener; a counsellor too was very much his role, just as it would have been for Ian Richardson.

Helen Richardson, the eldest daughter of Ian and Joan, was very taken with Catriona as a baby and she was our most reliable babysitter. She would come to visit us week after week, whether we were going out or not, and for this I was extremely grateful. A more fitting person I could not have found to be Catriona's godmother and I was genuinely pleased when Helen accepted my request.

One of the many times that Helen came for the whole day was when we were providing our grounds for an open-air concert in order to raise money for Alison Kinnaird and her Scottish music group Bradan Breach, to enable them to go to a folk festival in Yugoslavia. I felt honoured to be involved in their promotion, because their music was distinctive, a tribute to the Scottish tradition. When I was in hospital having Catriona, Alison lent me her knee harp so that I could play to my newly-born baby and also keep myself amused in between feeds! Alison is also a very well-known glass engraver and during that stay in hospital we organised a drawing of Glentruim to be engraved on a piece of rock crystal for me to give to Euan on our wedding anniversary that year. It has been our pride and joy, sitting on the drawing room mantlepiece ever since.

On the occasion of the open-air concert, apart from the midges, it was a fine evening with an audience which included both young and old from villages as far as Aviemore. It was held on the gravel outside the front door, which was suitably level for benches and chairs. With a bank on one side and the house on the other, the venue was well sheltered from evening winds.

Being summer, it was light for most of the concert and thankfully, it was only after all were seated that my peacocks gave their retirement call before hopping from branch to branch up the tallest tree. The younger birds would take a lower branch each, the oldest male, being last to roost, would take the highest perch and then they would all settle for the night.

Helen was in the nursery with Catriona during the concert and so had a grandstand view over the musicians, with voice and Scottish music resounding off the granite walls. Pipes, clarsach, fiddle, flute and song were part of the entertainment given by these talented young people and it was a spectacular evening. The necessary funding was raised for the players, which enabled them to fulfil their ambition – to perform in Yugoslavia.

When Ian Richardson retired it was decided that a locum was to be placed in the local practice while the Health Board interviewed suitable candidates for the full-time post. This was advertised three times and two candidates were shortlisted. The first choice did not turn up for his first day: it was later discovered that he was a registered nurse and not a medical practitioner at all. The second was from England and he took a month to turn the job down.

In the meantime we were allocated a locum, who was later nicknamed Dr Dram! He was a large man with a beard and a face that portrayed his love for whisky. He would arrive at your doorstep in his old Bentley with his labrador at his side – it accompanied him everywhere, even to the bedside. Unfortunately, when calls came in out of surgery hours, his secretary would have to call the pubs, one by one, before contacting him for the emergency!

However, Dr Dram did have followers who wished him to stay and take on the full-time post in the area. A petition for this went round from house to house, written on the back of a cornflakes packet! Then there were those who just did not like to lose yet another public service in the area. For instance, Laggan used to have its own policeman around 1900 – Mr MacDonald, who patrolled the area on his bicycle. Laggan also had its own post office, which was merely a wee tin shed, but served the purpose well until it was closed. Then, the district nurse had to be re-housed in Newtonmore, because of the dampness in her house in Laggan. So to lose a resident doctor would be the last amenity gone apart from the school.

Sheena Slimon was one of the district nurses at the time of Dr Dram and she told me that one morning he had called her out for an emergency. This was for old Crookie, the shepherd who lived at Balnahard, not far from Glentruim. Crookie had been poaching fish in milk over the stove for his supper. While he was waiting for it to cook he sat down with a dram and had fallen asleep, during which time the milk had boiled over and had consequently extinguished the gas flame. When Crookie woke, he noticed that there was no flame on the gas so immediately lit it. There followed a huge explosion. The house was blown to bits and Crookie plus dog were thrown free on to the ground beyond the cottage. He picked himself up and went immediately to his neighbour, where I believe his understatement was, 'There has been a wee bit of a bang!'

Seeing the demolished cottage, everyone thought that Crookie and his dog would have perished. However, he and his dog were found to be well, apart from the odd graze on Crookie's back.

Our next resident doctor was Donald Fraser, who had, before this post, been in a few practices in Scotland, including Lossiemouth, where Donald and his family had lived close to the airfield. Donald told me that when he looked out of the window every morning, he used to think, 'This is the place for a hydrogen bomb!' With this thought in mind the Frasers decided to move from Lossiemouth and Donald found a post in Nova Scotia, but longed to return to Scotland. Finally, after our third attempt to fill the post in Laggan, Donald was accepted as our local doctor.

The nearest to a bomb Donald would get to in Laggan was when the jets came swooping down through the valley, engaged in low-range practice. We used to think that they focused on the tower of Glentruim, using it as turning point, when they zoomed up and around it before returning back to base. The noise was sudden and disturbing. Euan consistently complained to the Ministry of Defence, once even asking them to exonerate him if the jets suddenly appeared in the site of his rifle while out shooting! Correspondence regarding this disturbance continued throughout the years, with little effect. The jet-planes would be so low that you could actually see the pilot in his cockpit, with the number clearly visible on the side of the plane. Travel being faster than the speed of sound, little wonder I grabbed a towel while in the bath one morning, when I saw a face followed quickly by the bang that shattered the window panes.

Donald, who seemed young to be a doctor, was tall and lean, with fair, bushy hair and a moustache, and his rimmed glasses added gravity to his already serious face. It takes years to be accepted in the Highlands, but it must have been even more intrepid for this young man to follow in the footsteps of such a well-loved and respected doctor as Ian.

No doubt there were comments made by patients, referring to what the Old Doctor would have done, but there were all sorts of other tangible reminders of this great man's way of life. The surgery garden was full of carcasses of deer, obviously buried there by Ian, and found when the Frasers were digging the garden, obviously buried there by Ian. There were even more when he brought the odd half stag in its pelt for the Frasers' deerhound. Then there would be yet another carcass to deal with!

No one escapes bad backs in the Highlands; there is always coal and wood to be brought in for the fires and heavy loads are unavoidable. It was a boon to Laggan when we all discovered Donald's expertise in backs; no longer did we have to travel to Inverness or Edinburgh for specialists. Donald was self-taught in back problems and once told me how he discovered his technique. It was purely by accident that he realised that there were things going on with the back that doctors did not know about. One day on a train to Inverness from Glasgow he had been suffering severe pain in the shoulder. As the train came to a stop, he grabbed the rail above him; suddenly his shoulder clicked and the pain was immediately relieved. Three years later, while working in Ayrshire in a mining town on a Saturday night, he was called out to a patient who was in severe pain from his shoulder. Donald prescribed painkillers, as had another doctor during the previous week, and then he left. However, on the way back he remembered the incident in the train. Turning back, he revisited his patient and went through the process for reducing a dislocated shoulder. When Donald called in the next day, he found his patient completely free from pain. Thereafter Donald extended his knowledge on back problems.

Donald preferred us to go to his surgery, but when he did visit us at home he told us that he often met our German guests, who had come for shooting, driving on the wrong side of the road. The back road through Glentruim is very narrow, with ditches either side, not many passing-places, serious bends and wildlife ready to get in your way. I never did expect to see anyone else when racing along to collect the children from school, or

*Top left.* Glentruim House
*Top right.* Hall
*Middle left.* Dining-room
*Middle right.* Smoking-room
*Bottom left.* Drawing-room

*Top.* Halfway House
*Middle.* Coach House
*Bottom.* Kennel Cottage

Burgener, ARTIST Harper, Kansas.

*Opposite top*. Shanval
*Opposite bottom*. Calum Piobair
*Above*. Norman, Euan's father, on right

Two character drawings of Euan by Johnnie Bruck

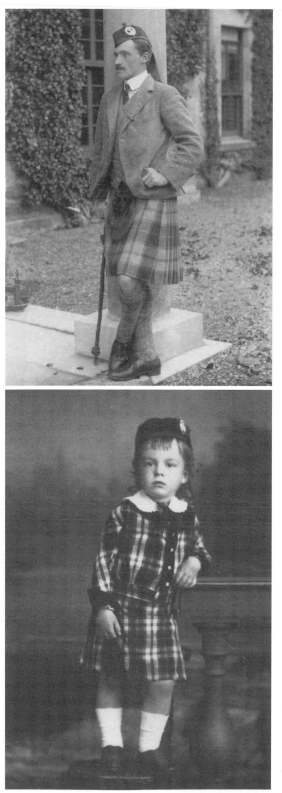

*Top*. Duncan, Euan's
uncle and husband
of Katie
*Bottom*. Euan's Uncle
Evan as a child

*Opposite*. Sandra and Euan on their wedding day, outside Perth Cathedral

*Top*. Euan's Aunt Eva

*Bottom*. Catriona sitting in front of the picture of Charlotte and Jane

Clan gathers outside Clan Macpherson house

Clan gathers after unveiling of cairn in memory of Ewan of the '45

*Top left*. Catriona and Lachlan at Newtonmore Games

*Top right*. Alex, Lachlan, Catriona, Bella and Charlie by the cannon on Glentruim lawn

*Bottom*. Sunday afternoon tea on Glentruim lawn during a clan gathering

*Back*. John McIntosh (piper), Meg, Alastair

*Middle*. Penny with Charlie, Euan, Sandra, Ronnie, Betty

*Front*. Alex, Bella, Catriona, Lachlan

*Top.* Euan, Bill and Alastair (left)
with Ormond Salvesen. Euan in front
*Bottom.* Euan and 'Bonnie' Bruck
posing for a picture

*Top.* Cannon being fired
on Glentruim lawn
*Bottom.* 'Broughy' enjoying
dessert after piping for guests

*Top*. Sandra playing the clarsach in the drawing room

*Bottom*. Euan looking across the valley

checking a holiday cottage; nor did Sheena Slimon, our neighbouring farmer's wife. Our cars would screech to an abrupt halt, we would exchange polite conversation and ultimately carry on with our journeys, leaving the only evidence of our encounter in skid-marks on the road. Sheena was one of the district nurses in the area; perhaps some of her journeys through Glentruim were more urgent than mine.

Peggy O'Reilly was the district nursing sister, midwife, health visitor and a Queen's nurse. Her area covered Laggan, Dalwhinnie, Newtonmore and often further afield. She was the second daughter of Thomas and Margaret Cattanach, a notable Newtonmore family, well-known to all in Badenoch. Peggy was a small lady with large, sad eyes and curly golden-brown hair, dedicated to her work, always kind, caring and helpful to everyone in the district. You would often meet her in the village and, no matter how busy she was, she would always stop to enquire after your health and your family. Her opening remarks were predictable: 'And how are you?' she would ask, with the emphasis on the 'are', in her good Badenoch accent, rarely heard today.

When I brought Catriona back from her birth at the hospital, not only was I inexperienced and nervous of my new baby, but I was alone. Without Peggy, I do not know how I would have managed. During those exhausting nights when I could not get Catriona settled, Peggy would be at the end of the telephone ready to give reassuring professional advice, even coming over to the house, late as it was, if she heard anxiety in my voice. She would brave the storm, however atrocious, then together we would pace the floor as the winds howled around the building. We would take turns to hold the baby in our arms, stopping only when a feed seemed appropriate, disregarding the fearsome cacophony outside.

All members of the local practice were well-liked and very much part of the community. They were expected to be on committees and involved with fund-raising issues and, furthermore, these busy people were always first to volunteer their services.

# 15

# *The Ceilidhs*

ONE cannot live in the Highlands without being involved in the traditional ceilidhs, which could be described as the spontaneous entertainment when crowds gather together. In the old days ceilidhs occurred within a gathering of friends or family members, with no television but plenty of whisky for the less bold. Over the years these have become more contrived and organised and are now well-established events held for visiting tourists.

One evening, when I was asked to play my clarsach at a ceilidh for tourists, held in the Mains Hotel in Newtonmore, I met Margaret Bennett, a notable Gaelic singer who had also been asked to take part. Most women are lucky if they have one aspect which makes them stand out in a crowd, whether beauty, character or even a certain 'je ne sais quoi'. Margaret was from Skye and seemed to have all these attributes. She had a strikingly beautiful face, was rich in charm, and spoke in the soft voice of the Islanders, pronouncing every syllable, which could captivate her audience as if spellbound. Her singing surpassed all others; the Gaelic songs were sung unaccompanied, according to tradition, and her guitar was brought out for the more contemporary pieces. Margaret worked at Kingussie School with children who required remedial teaching (though she was a highly qualified folklorist with a PhD). Later her career changed and vastly expanded when she moved to Edinburgh to work for the School of Scottish Studies. Before long, Margaret had written numerous books and subsequently travelled widely, in Britain and abroad, giving talks and lectures, and of course singing. She has often been invited to star on television and radio, and her many publications are proof of her success.

Margaret and I instantly became close friends and thereafter performed together with clarsach and song in ceilidhs throughout Badenoch. My favourite venue was at home, at Glentruim, where the true traditional ceilidhs became very much part of our lives.

One of my more memorable ceilidhs at Glentruim followed a champagne dinner I had provided for a group of young ladies from Aultmore Finishing School for Girls. Many of them were daughters of diplomats from all over the world. It was to be the highlight of their visit, and this evening certainly lived up to their expectations.

Aultmore is situated at the north-east side of Nethybridge, a neo-Georgian harled mansion, built in 1912–14 for the owner of a Moscow department store. This exquisite building was designed by C.H.B Quennell and was surrounded by well-kept gardens. It was the girls' last week of the term at Aultmore and most of them had scant knowledge about Highland tradition and music. They arrived by bus, along with the owners of the school, Major and Mrs Hargreaves. Our piper, Mr Brough, was poised for their arrival across the other side of the drive in front of the entrance to Glentruim and his first slow air must have been heard for miles across the valley on such a peaceful summer's night.

We fondly referred to our piper as 'Broughy', and he well deserved to be on local postcards, for he was the perfect figure of a Scottish piper. He lived on the outskirts of Aviemore in a little cottage and his main employment was with British Rail. When we took the sleeper to London, we were often privileged to have Broughy look after us. Indeed, I recall that on one notable return journey, having had to run for the train after a very good bank lunch, Broughy kept the carriage door open a short time longer than scheduled so that we would not be left behind!

Broughy, a rounded, kilted gentleman, whose full cheeks toned nicely with the deep red of his tartan, blew the pipes with gusto. His plaid was strategically draped over one shoulder as he marched up and down in time to his tunes, trying to ignore the nips of the intrepid midges on his bare white knees! It was only when the piping stopped that we could tell how determined the midges had been. Broughy's scratching became too urgent to be discreet!

It was formal dress and the girls looked stunning in their grand ball gowns, each gloved hand outstretched for ours as they entered. They looked slightly intimidated by the towering mansion and the grandeur within. Some spoke broken English, but others struggled to say anything at all.

My twin sister Zoë and her very dashing husband Johnnie, an airline pilot, were staying with us at the time. They too shook hands with our guests in the hall as our housekeeper took coats, wraps and shawls before guiding everyone towards the drawing-room.

Our guests were offered glasses of champagne as they entered the drawing-room. Then, as we congregated around the fire, Euan formally welcomed everyone with a few chosen words.

The girls were fascinated by Euan, who was quite the Highland chieftain, wearing dress Macpherson tartan and black evening Prince Charlie jacket with silver buttons. His whole attire had first belonged to his great-grandfather and the old dyes on the kilt were delicately faded in comparison with the modern colours. His plaid over the left shoulder was long and complicated to adjust. I always had to assist him with this, taking it round his back and then to the front through a loop. The plaid brooch was one of a kind, having a large silver back with a sizeable yellow Cairngorm stone in the middle. A powder-horn, also trimmed with silver and Cairngorms, hung from his waist on a silver chain, pointing down to an ornate sgian-dubh, which peeped above one of his hand-knitted dress tartan kilt-socks. These kilt socks were one hundred years old. The family sgian-dubh was in itself a sheath, housing a silver fork and knife, both with Cairngorms at the top. The sporran was also a showpiece, looking like a long white beard with three black hair tassels and an intricate silver top. Like Broughy, Euan's picture was in many books and magazines all over the world – as an example of an archetypal Highland chieftain.

The crackling of flames within the large, white marble fireplace broke the odd silences, while words comprehensible to those who were not so fluent in the English language were sought. How refreshing it was to see Margaret and her son Martyn arrive to break up the rather stilted conversation. Johnnie had no problem with conversation, given such a young and attractive audience: he had always had a way with the girls. But my sister was having a less easy time!

Martyn was about ten years old then, and had already mastered the pipes to perfection. Now he is one of Scotland's most talented young composers, and also played several instruments to audiences of thousands of people. He was in great demand and his recordings and volume of CDs soon far overtook those of his mother. The first time I heard him play, when he was very young, was in his own home standing on the kitchen table, his little body struggling with the weight of the pipes, the vastness of this instrument obscuring his tiny frame. Because of his stature, the only way he could manage to tune the drones was if he turned the pipes upside down, to reach the valves. He learnt quickly, was a natural musician and his skills soon extended to an accumulation of instruments.

We were all piped into dinner and, after a good dram, Broughy was thanked by us all and then was off home. The dining-room table groaned with food: a whole salmon dressed with slices of lemon, aspic and parsley; a glazed ham; and a shoulder of venison. There was every salad you could imagine, which helped to fill the table, and sideboards held tempting sweets such as Pavlova, meringues, chocolate mousse, brandy-snaps and éclairs. A whole Stilton and oatcakes were also on a smaller table by the door which led into the butler's pantry, and a bottle of port sat there too for those who dared.

Euan's great-grandparents, grandparents, aunts and uncles looked down from the portraits on the peach gloss-painted walls, their eyes seeming to follow one's every move. It was almost dark when the heavy braided scarlet curtains were pulled to embrace us within this candle-lit room of history. Great lengths of wood burned in the iron fire-basket, which had received a fresh coat of black-lead that very morning. The mantel and surround were of black marble, on top of which stood figurines of horses with their reins held by young boys. The only other ornament between these figurines was a black marble mantel clock, similar to the one in the smoking-room. For this particular evening, the table had also been turned and stood to one side of the room, which gave space for the entertainment that was to follow after dinner.

Good food and wine, the flickering of light from the fire, the red candles quietly dripping into their silver candle-holders and candelabras, combined with spontaneous laughter set the scene for a happy evening. At the start of the ceilidh we were joined by a young Highland dancer from the village with her own piper and also by Margaret Sharp, who was to sing. Margaret lived in Laggan with her husband Donnie, who was a gamekeeper on one of the neighbouring estates. He often used to help us out in the busy shooting season and also during the burning of the heather. He was quite a character.

The precise footwork of the dancer had the girls in raptures, the Highland fling and the sword dance being well practiced. Later Margaret Sharp sang a few songs, which were much appreciated, and I played the clarsach, an instrument the girls had never heard before, the sound of which delighted them. Then came little Martyn's turn. He stood on a small table and his playing was unsurpassed, utterly enchanting. His mother sang next and told wonderful tales between songs and it was no surprise that everyone sat motionless. After this, Margaret Bennett sang while I played the harp and our guests were encouraged to join in the Gaelic chorus. Then came the big moment when guests were invited to participate with their party-piece.

By then the girls were sitting in a semicircle, some on chairs and others on cushions on the floor. My brother-in-law Johnnie lapped up their flirtations and, with a smile on his face and a wicked look in his eye, he was the first to volunteer. I could feel the heat creeping up my neck into my face, which must have turned as scarlet as the curtains when Johnnie started singing the chorus from 'The Ball of Kirriemuir': 'Four-and-twenty virgins came down from Inverness, and when the ball was over there were four-and-twenty less.' Every word was meticulously pronounced and horribly distinct. My clarsach was not large enough to hide my embarrassment and Margaret (Martyn's mother), who was sitting beside me, like myself, wished to be swallowed up by the floor. Dawn Hargreaves threw me a look of horror and Charles Hargreaves tried to hide his amusement. The girls, laughed and hummed the tune, but I think the innuendoes in the song escaped most of them. Euan's piercing Macpherson brown eyes were wide, his beard pointing upwards, as he pursed his lips, a familiar expression of rage to those who knew him.

Polite words of thanks were given as the party, one by one, said goodbye before wearily climbing back into the bus. After a head count we were informed that one girl was missing. In unison both my sister and I demanded, 'Where's Johnnie?'

The next day I was telephoned by the school and accusations were made by the missing girl. Johnnie laughingly said, 'I should be so lucky!', and the subject was avoided for the rest of the day.

Fortunately, in the evening the atmosphere was cleared when the school telephoned once more to say that the girl in question had been found with an empty half-bottle of vodka in her large evening bag, and had also admitted to fabrication.

# 16

# *Clan Gatherings*

THE annual Clan Gathering took place during the first weekend of August, but before the arrival of our Macpherson cousins I would always be found sitting at the kitchen table, making new kilts for the children. Because the children grew out of their kilts so quickly, I could not justify buying new ones until they were older. Our ottomans gradually filled with handmade kilts and tartan skirts of varying sizes! No kilts were ever discarded – the older the better! Some of Euan's, handed down from past generations, though slightly threadbare, were still very service-able.

The long and narrow pine kitchen table in the middle of the room had been the surface for numerous activities over the years, apart from its primary purpose: sewing, mending china, children's play activities, preparing game, and even skinning roe deer. Once, while I was expecting Lachlan, I found a roe deer hanging in the larder. The gamekeeper had been taken ill and, hating waste, there was no alternative for me but to deal with the carcass myself. Just as I was cutting up the roe at the kitchen table, with a hatchet and saw, there was a loud knock on the back door. Absentmindedly, with tool still in hand, I answered the door to the coalman. I apologised for my appearance and explained what I was doing, but the sight of the bloodied hatchet and a young woman heavily pregnant left him speechless. His blackened face turned white!

For weeks running before the Gathering, the kitchen table was in continual use. I would be preparing the baking and any meals which could be made in advance were then frozen in our very large freezer. A large ham, a whole salmon, haunch of venison, game lasagne, 'coronation rabbit', together with a selection of sweets and numerous pieces of shortbread were part of the weekend's menu.

Game was free for us; sides of beef, pork or legs of lamb were a luxury. We were extremely appreciative when my friend Vicky and her family came to stay bringing beef joints, for we had almost forgotten the taste of such meat. A can-opener was a tool rarely used in my kitchen; what could not be grown or shot was not on the daily menu. Even the dogs lived on offal from game or scraps from our plates mixed with dog-meal. Through necessity I became quite a dab hand at disguising game, because our family became so tired of it.

Before our guests for the Gathering arrived, the kitchen window would be wide open, allowing gentle breezes in to cool me in my frantic race against time to make the kilts. A large yew tree stood to the left of the window, but apart from this there was an unobstructed view down over the lawns, the fields, and then across the valley towards the Cairngorm mountains. During pauses from sewing I would enjoy this view.

Behind the yew tree there was a shed, in which I kept grain for my peafowl, but the grain unfortunately attracted rats, which were a great nuisance. The rats were destructive and what they could get up to was incredible. One time they made a hole, only about two inches wide, in the top of a cupboard in the back corridor and I actually watched a rat pull one of Euan's thick woolly jumpers down through this small space!

At the Gatherings, you could always count on Ronnie and Betty Macpherson, from Comrie, to be our first guests. Indeed, as years passed by, their holiday would extend and they would arrive on the Thursday or perhaps the Wednesday, instead of the

Friday. Ronnie wore a perpetual smile on his face, even when Betty, who was older, bossed him about and scolded him incessantly. Clan Gatherings would never be the same without these two; they were loyal and staunch members of the clan. Ronnie had a rotund figure, round face with a moustache, and clear rimless glasses. He enjoyed life to the full. Betty also had a generous figure, but was the more serious of the pair. They would come to stay laden with cheeses from a well-known cheese shop in Comrie.

As long as he was chieftain of the Newtonmore Games, Ormond Salvesen was in the habit of arriving on the Friday in preparation for the Games on Saturday. His house-gift was a box of kippers from the Isle of Man, where he lived, or a whole fillet of beef, which he himself would cook. He insisted on cooking the beef rare, and rightly so!

After a few years of Ormond's customary visits to Glentruim, we had the pleasure of meeting his third wife Jean, whom we were delighted to welcome into our Gathering party. We had heard a great deal about Jean from Ormond; 'She has a heart of gold' he kept telling us before we met her. Jean was perfect for Ormond as they had so much in common – their mutual bar opened for the day about eleven in the morning!

The provisions for the weekend would be further augmented by raspberries from Blairgowrie, brought by the Cluny Macphersons, who normally arrived in time for lunch on the Friday, as did the Pitmain Macphersons. Latterly, the Pitmains travelled over from Achara on the west coast of Scotland, but before they acquired this estate they had to travel up from London. Our festivities were always enriched by copious quantities of whisky and wine, which appeared at different times during the weekend from the recipients of our Highland hospitality.

When all of the Macpherson children were young, each of these weekends at Glentruim was memorable in one way or the other. William Macpherson 'Cluny' and his wife Sheila had three children with them: Annie, Alan and Jamie. Alastair Macpherson 'Pitmain' and his wife Penny brought with them Bella, Alexander and Charlie, the youngest, who was my godchild. Glentruim would be bursting at the seams with every bedroom occupied, including those in the tower.

Bill (William Macpherson) was a High Court judge in London, distinguished both in work and in appearance, a tall, fit-looking man. Sheila, always at his side, had a charming personality, and was as dedicated to the clan, as was her husband.

Alastair and his wife Penny too made a handsome couple, both tall, attractive and fun to be with. Euan and Penny first met at the bar in the Duke of Gordon Hotel at the Clan Ball, during the Pitmains' first rally. Penny was gasping for a drink and this was noted by Euan, who promptly did the necessary. We got on exceptionally well from our introduction to each other and from that initial meeting we invited them to Glentruim for the Clan Gatherings. From the time everyone arrived, one could hardly draw breath; the weekend was packed with entertainment. Macphersons came from all over the world and for their benefit smaller events, between the major ones, began to multiply as the years went on.

Some time early on the Friday morning I would go into Kingussie to the Wright Style Salon to have my hair done by Gwynneth. Gwynneth would tell me which Macpherson ladies had booked in for the day and I would meet up with a few while I was there. This was my only time of relaxation before the end of the weekend. Then, after lunch, there was the council meeting for the few involved. The Macpherson men in our party, being members of the council, would have to leave as soon as they had finished the last morsel of their sweet. The ladies, however, would carry on with wine, in the smoking-room, and catch up with news and gossip.

The sun never failed us during the Gatherings, making it almost too hot for the men in their heavy kilts. Unfortunately, these spells of heat caused problems with our domestic water supply, which came from two springs on the hill. Droughts never failed to coincide with this busiest weekend in the year and everyone had to be instructed to use water sparingly. Our guests, therefore, had to be reminded not to leave the tap running while brushing their teeth, and only to flush loos when absolutely necessary! The children shared baths and the ladies took advantage of the men being late back from the council meetings and drew their baths first, before dressing for the Macpherson ball in the evening.

Having looked at old photographs of past balls, we kept up the tradition of taking group shots outside the front door, before leaving for the ball. There were two photographs to be taken, the first as normal, the second with everyone turned around for a picture of the backs! There was not a dramatically noticeable sign of age in the front views but, as years passed, it was more perceptible on the back views, by the gradual receding hair of the gentlemen! Then, as the children became of a suitable age, they too joined the group.

At the ball in the Duke of Gordon Hotel in Kingussie, Bill and Sheila, along with the current chairman and his wife would shake hands with their clan members as they arrived for the cocktails. The ball would then begin. It was always stirring to see the dancers, all clad in kilts or ballgowns with tartan sashes – a truly authentic clan ball. Charlie Miller at the Duke of Gordon Hotel always made sure that we were all well looked after and his staff produced an excellent buffet during the evening.

In the early days, we started the ball with the Grand March, headed by the Clunys and followed by us – the Glentruims – and the Pitmains, with all other members following on. When the numbers increased over the years, the march had to be withdrawn. The ball, however, was unique, with everyone being so friendly and enjoying the contact with each other as if they had never been away. A closer clan one could not imagine and the whole weekend was of a kind that allowed members to be totally relaxed, enjoying the company of their extended family.

Every minute together was taken advantage of and every event had a party after the party. After the ball, in the Glentruim drawing-room, it would sometimes be daylight before we retired. With no more driving required, the evening tended to lead to yet more drinking, inspired stories and antics. Ronnie, while being scrutinised by Betty, would dance the sword dance, with crossed matches on the floor instead of swords. His movements and his weight, which would cause the very room to shake, would have us all in fits of laughter. Bill also had his party piece, which involved balancing a glass of water and singing a song while he bobbed up and down. Euan would recite poetry and, if not too tired, I would play the harp and perhaps sing.

It was the annual general meeting on the Saturday morning and for some it could be a struggle to keep eyes open, let alone agree 'aye' at the correct moment. Sitting in rows in Newtonmore village hall, we heard about the achievements of members belonging to the Macpherson branches all over the world. Enthusiasm was apparent, with everyone obviously proud to be a member of the clan. Bill always ended each meeting with his own words of encouragement and thanks to his clan. I, however, would be sitting there worrying about the time. There was never enough of it to get home and prepare the lunch before the departure to the Newtonmore Highland Games and the Macpherson March.

Then it was back for lunch to Glentruim, where Ormond and Jean would be waiting; not being Macphersons, they were able to have long lie-ins and their pre-lunch drinks would have already commenced. I remember one lunch in particular when, on my return, I was greeted by Jean coming down the whole length of the staircase on her bottom. She picked herself up gracefully and laughed away her bruises. Euan's late Uncle Duncan was less lucky when he fell head-first down these stairs, breaking a bone in his neck and then ending his days in a bed in the smoking-room.

Jean had another mishap after this lunch when, helping to take platters of food to the kitchen, she was carrying a large ham which was too heavy for her. It slid off the ashette and skidded across the polished surrounds to meet me coming through the pantry door. We all laughed, and then it was all haste to get to the Games in time.

Only the men took part in the Macpherson March and as soon as our male children were able to walk, they too joined in. It was an impressive occasion. They would march from Old Ralia, a house which was a short distance from the gamesfield on the old A9. Then the traffic would be halted by the police, while our chief led his men with his chieftains, Euan and Alastair, by his side. They were closely followed by banner-bearers, then the rest of the male contingent, as they marched down the road and into the gamesfield. This march would be headed by a Scottish pipe band. Close at hand, the Macpherson ladies, plus their children, mostly in tartan, would be standing at the other side of the gamesfield fence as they watched proudly, cameras clicking. There were the same photographs every year – only the rapid growth of the children, signs of grey hair and a few expanding waistlines could identify the years, and would not have been noticed unless documented. But longshot snaps were kind to wrinkles and lines in faces!

In front of Glentruim, on the top lawns, was a pair of cannons which we had proof-fired in Chatham. We used to fire these cannons on special occasions, one of which, naturally, was the Newtonmore Games and Clan March. We had to have our own gun team to look after the cannons and they had to be specifically trained for their firing – blanks of course.

It was customary that I presented the silver trophies to the Highland Dancers. This made it compulsory for me to stay to the bitter end. I would stand on the platform while the dancers curtsied or bowed, shaking each hand while murmuring pleasantries; then my deed would be done. The dancers came from all over Scotland and I would watch their progress each year with great interest. By this time other members of the clan would have started the 'happy hour' in the Clan Museum. It was a convivial hour of drinking whisky for those who enjoyed a dram, the members packed into the main room like sardines.

The ceilidih was the next event to get ready for and the children came too. We were lucky if we had as much as an hour to get home from the museum, turn around and go back to the Duke of Gordon. These ceilidhs were too organised for my liking; I preferred those of a more spontaneous nature. But they were a treat for those from abroad, some of whom had never heard instruments such as the clarsach, which I sometimes played during the evening.

The ceilidh after the ceilidh was easily the most relaxed event that took place, when we all congregated in the bar later that evening. Serious drinking took place at this 'proper' ceilidh. This was when hair was well and truly let down, and inhibitions were freely abandoned.

The Sunday was, for me, the most exhausting day of the year. We would erect a marquee in the garden so that the whole clan could come for afternoon tea. A vast quantity of home-made cakes and biscuits were prepared well in advance, which meant I filled all of my tins and the second deep-freeze. The other and larger of the two deep-freezes, incidentally, was constantly full of bags containing unplucked birds and wildcats (before they were protected), which were waiting to be made into sporrans. At the afternoon tea, Macphersons could catch up with those they had not had time to talk to over the fast-moving preceding days.

Anne Bain, Isobel Carr and often Vicky Thain would come to help me with the tea party. Suzie Curtis, if she was at home, would be there too, always amused at how we used to lower the large heavy teapots on ropes out of the kitchen window. 'The tea bags are like small pillows', she would say!

It was wonderful to see children of various sizes running around the lawns enjoying themselves while Bruce Macpherson marched up and down playing the pipes. Bruce had performed thus on the Glentruim lawns from a very early age, his progress over the years a delight to watch. The cannons would be fired, and those standing too close would cover their ears as we all gazed at the smoke softly dispersing into the distance, after which the briefly interrupted conversation could continue. This gentle afternoon, with no rush to be at any other event, was perhaps a perfect ending to a hectic weekend.

It took days to recover from these weekends; then plans would be put in motion for the following year, which always came round all too soon! It was a weekend firmly booked in the Macpherson calendar, a weekend never to be missed unless distance or job dictated otherwise.

Macpherson Clan Gatherings take place all over the world. Bill and Sheila went to many, as did other members of the clan in Scotland, but Euan and I only went to one in the USA. On Friday 13 September 1985 Euan and I flew from Prestwick. It was a typical Friday 13th, with disaster from beginning to end. Driving down early in the morning from Glentruim, we were confronted with roadworks throughout the journey. We caught the plane only in the nick of time, our bulging suitcases having been opened, with the dirks and sgian-dubhs queried. With a tight schedule, we knew that we would be lucky if we arrived in time for the reception before dinner. We were, however, to be met at the airport, which would hasten the last part of our journey. The flight passed smoothly up until about the last hour, when a Glasgow man, well inebriated, became over-friendly with an air hostess. He was asked to sit down, but carried on with groping hands. Finally the captain himself had to come to the rescue but he unfortunately received a punch on the nose. We were diverted to Canada, so that the unruly passenger from Glasgow could be arrested. He was also forced to wear a straitjacket in one of the

138

front seats for the rest of the journey. Arriving in Canada, there were further delays while the police came to make the arrest and to check the aircraft for drugs.

How nice it was at last to arrive safely and to be whisked away by a shiny black limousine bearing little Scottish and American flags on the bonnet. We had been exhausted but were then treated like VIPs, which almost made up for the terrible journey.

In every year that ends with a five or a zero, Canada and the USA join together for their Macpherson Clan Gathering. The year we visited was no exception; the venue was Greenville Village in Dearborn. Cluny, our chief, attended with Sheila, together with the Pitmains, Alastair and Penny. Sandy and Catherine Macpherson from Edinburgh were also there. Sandy was our secretary of the Clan Association at the time and his whole family have always been great supporters, assisting with a great many aspects of clan business and events (Bruce, their son mentioned previously, piped at the Glentruim tea parties).

In America the usual run of events took place, including a reception followed by a banquet. This particular evening went as planned, apart from the absence of the first course, which should have been haggis. Prohibited from importing haggis, the local butcher had made them himself for the dinner, but unfortunately his van broke down on the way to the hotel! A courier was sent to rescue the haggis, which were frozen and resembled little cannonballs. The meal had to commence, with speeches between each course, while the chef boiled the solid haggis and then our national dish was finally presented, addressed and taken after the dessert! By that time everyone was thoroughly enjoying themselves and was not put out at all, unlike the organiser who was getting hotter by the minute. Euan and I did enjoy most of this trip, but it had turned out to be tiring and sometimes stressful! Nevertheless, it was an extraordinary experience for us both.

The jubilee year was 1996, when the Macphersons celebrated

their fiftieth Clan Rally. At the time the Chairman of the Association was Ewen Macpherson, from Perthshire, who efficiently carried out the mammoth task of organising this special occasion. Bruce, his secretary, recruited many of the younger members, those under twenty-five, to assist with events. It was a huge success, reputed moreover to be the largest gathering of any clan since Culloden. This was undoubtedly due to the contribution from the young committee, supervised by Bruce, and the endless hours of hard work undertaken by Ewen and his wife Margaret.

Euan and I donated in perpetuity a plot of land to the clan Macpherson during the Jubilee Clan Rally, the site of which is above Shanvall, a magnificent and noble viewpoint overlooking the upper Spey Valley. It was the intention to build a cairn in memory of Cluny Macpherson of the Forty-Five Rebellion. Because Cluny had died in Dunkirk, his precise place of burial unknown, it was thus befitting that there should be some sort of memorial to him which clan members could visit. The building of the cairn was a great cooperative effort: John Barton carried out the necessary conveyance for free, as did architect Robert Macpherson (son-in-law of Ewen and Margaret). Cheques for the construction and stones for the cairn were donated by Macphersons from all over the world, with stones even sent from places as remote as the Great Wall of China and the bottom of the North Sea. It was a very moving occasion when Bill, our chief, unveiled the cairn that August day in 1996.

The bond that Macphersons have is galvanised from the top, our chief and his wife keeping us a strong and vibrant clan. Macphersons, our children and our children's children, generation after generation, will find cousins within this extended family all over the world, always with a welcome in their homes.

# 17

# The Two Sisters

WHEN Euan and I slept in 'The Army Bedroom', so named after the presence of the Marching Army, Catriona at the age of three slept in one of the small rooms off our shared corridor. Beside her room was another small one, which was Lachlan's as soon as he had outgrown the cot in the nursery. These two rooms side by side made ideal children's bedrooms, and they even had a quaint little narrow door between them, with brass handles on either side. This door was left open at night, so that Catriona could reassure her little brother if he got scared in the dark. The house being full of strange things, it was not unusual for Lachlan to dash through that open door and creep into his sister's bed. Catriona once related a time such as this, when Lachlan raced through to her in the night. 'Trina, Trina,' his words tripping him and voice hardly coherent, 'There was a light – and then it was gone, and there was another light – and then it was gone!' He was in her bed within seconds. Catriona said that she had never believed that fear could cause hair to stand on end, as one says, until that moment. She told me that Lachlan's face was ashen as his little shaking body got in beside her, and every strand of hair was standing straight up – on end! Catriona said that she had often seen lights coming and going, but had got used to it.

Catriona was about three years old when her screams would waken the whole household during the night and I would have to go down the steps from our bedroom to hers to calm her.

141

Entering her room, I would find her sitting bolt upright in bed patting the bedclothes. She would be very distressed, crying, 'It wasn't me, I promise it wasn't me – it wasn't me,' which she repeated constantly. These nightmares went on for a long time, in exactly the same way each night, with the same actions and the same words.

Catriona enjoyed having a piggy-back from her father on the way up to bed and sometimes Euan would prolong this game, through the public rooms, before going up the front stairs. Into the drawing-room they would go, and as they reached the picture on the wall of Charlotte and Jane, Euan's great-grandaunts, they would stop. Looking at Jane on the left of the picture, Catriona would say 'That's me!' Then the journey to bed would be completed. When visitors saw the picture, they would say to Catriona, 'That is a lovely drawing of you on the left, but who is on the right?' 'That is my friend,' Catriona would reply. Jane must have been about the same age as Catriona when the picture was drawn.

Charlotte and Jane grew up together and lived in a large house on Glentruim, called Crubin, in the area of Crubenmore. Neither of them married and they remained in the same house all their days. On 16 November 1866 their housekeeper, Emily MacDonald, had been walking into Kingussie, which was in those days the nearest village, to fetch the shopping. Newtonmore had not been built but was developed later as the 'new town on the moor'. Emily, who had been in service with the two sisters for eighteen years, had looked back and seen smoke billowing up over Crubenmore. Rushing back she had found Crubin House burnt to a cinder. Along with the house the two sisters had perished.

It seemed too much of a coincidence to us that, firstly, Catriona looked so like Jane, and that secondly she acted as if she were patting out a fire in her bed during her nightmares. Was this tragedy the source of her nightmares? I asked Catriona about her dreams and she told me that in these dreams she knew that she was in her own house, but that it was not Glentruim, and that there was a fire. She also felt a strong sense of guilt, but qualified this by saying, 'It was not my fault.'

Yet again I searched the library for information about Euan's great-grandaunts. I uncovered a large old book with Gaelic at the front and the translation into English at the back. The book was by Reverend Thomas Sinton, published in Inverness in 1906. There was a poem in it, written by Emily, the housekeeper, and it described her setting out to Kingussie and then looking back on the fatal incident. But one line translated to the effect, 'The fault was on Miss Charlotte – that 'twas she'!

I sat with Catriona, read the poem to her, and we discussed the whole tragic affair. I told her my thoughts on the matter. I felt that through Catriona, who looked so like her forebear, Jane was telling us that it was not her who had caused herself and her sister to be tragically burned in the fire that fatal afternoon. How Emily claimed to know the true facts we will never know. Who or what had started the fire was never recorded.

A house named Crubenbeg was built on the site and this too burnt down just over a hundred years later, in November 1968. The McCormack family had been living there during the second incident but mercifully nobody was hurt. I heard from Eileen, Mrs McCormack's daughter, that she and her mother had been out feeding the horses when the house mysteriously caught fire. She told me that, many years previously, her great-uncle had added new bay windows of pitch pine to the front of the house; once they had caught fire, it was a matter of minutes before the whole house went up in flames. That evening when Eileen returned home after feeding the horses, she found that she was unable to open the front door because of the smoke. It must have been a heartbreaking experience for them. Although their close friends and neighbours, Johnnie and Ishbel MacBean, helped them to salvage some of the drawing-room furniture, much was lost in the fire, including many of Eileen's wedding presents.

Poor Mrs McCormack was left with only the garments she stood up in that horrific night.

Thinking back on her memorable days at Crubenbeg, Eileen told me that one night she and her mother were sitting in the kitchen when, seeing the quizzical look on her daughter's face, she said, 'Have you been hearing that too?' For a long time they had both heard footsteps in the bedroom above, but neither had uttered a word!

Eileen eventually went to live further north, but her brother Terry and his wife remained in the area and started a mobile car repair service, later expanding this business when they purchased a garage in Kingussie. We were among their first customers.

Charlotte and Jane's graveyard can be sighted from the main road north through the Highlands and is not far from the River Truim. Euan and I often used to explore the ruins of Crubenbeg, which sat above the graveyard. Evidence of the last fire still remained: charred beams leaned precariously over half-demolished walls and flooring stood over nothing but rubble. The odd rusty pot, china jar or blue medicine-bottle were part of the remnants to be found, but it was a hazardous place to search.

A short time later, I chatted to Catriona about the fire which had taken the lives of Charlotte and Jane. I also reminded Euan about the poem written by Emily, the housekeeper who had looked after the two old ladies. This prompted him to go over to the graveyard on the other side of the estate in order to tend the sisters' graves. I was tired and had a bad cold so stayed at home, but Euan went with the children and our bank manager, Carnegie Brown, and his wife Marjorie, who came from Alnwick. I remember so well the conversations we had over dinner, the first time they came to stay. They were both very much involved in community life, and we heard about their village activities and the local fairs. Baking, home produce and even vegetables seemed to be exhibited and entered into competitions. I could not imagine how one could get excited about the largest marrow or the biggest tomato, for instance, but Marjorie made it all sound riveting.

When they reached the graveyard the gate was locked because the key had never been found since we came to Glentruim. Euan jumped over the railings which encompassed this resting-place of only two graves, the graves of the sisters. He then promptly cleared up bits of fallen wood, 'this and that', as he described it to me, to make the place look kept. Catriona was running around, with her long fair hair blowing in the wind, and all the time Euan was watching her, he was reminded of Jane. 'I kept thinking of Jane', he said to me on his return.

Finishing his clearing up, he walked back to the Range Rover, where Lachlan sat, cuddled up asleep in Marjorie's arms. Euan opened the boot, in which he placed his tools, then, when he slammed the door shut and started the engine, Lachlan woke. Lachlan sat up and looked out of the window. His eyes moved and his finger moved, and his words were clear as he spoke to his father: 'Daddy, see the lady. Daddy, Daddy, see the lady. See the lady.' Euan drove away and they all sat in silence. 'A very strange feeling,' Euan said.

My immediate reaction was that we must go back and we must tend the graves. From that day, Catriona was rid of her nightmares: the past had been laid to rest. Jane, having made her statement, was free of the unfounded guilt which she seemed to be expressing through Catriona.

It is quite normal for a child to have an imaginary friend to play with, and Catriona was no exception. But I wondered whether her 'friend' was a figment of her imagination, or was it her 'sister', when she lived for a short time in the life belonging to Jane?

The story of Catriona and Jane was later told in a documentary produced by ITV during the winter of 1994. The programme was called *The Strange Show*, with Margaret Bennett as the interviewer. Euan, Catriona and I were interviewed in the first half and we talked about the fire. The second part of the documentary was taken outside Glentruim, when snow was falling, where Margaret asked Euan and Catriona about the incident at the graveyard. It ended with a short film, with a young actress representing Catriona.

The old Glentruim Schoolhouse was very close to Crubenbeg, and, according to Ishbel MacBean, Aunt Katie did a great deal for the benefit of the children there, often visiting for a chat. She loved the young and was well-known for her support and involvement in the Girl Guide organisation; there was even an area beyond the Invernahavon fields on Glentruim made available by Katie for a Girl Guide camp.

Up until the 1950s Glentruim Schoolhouse was going strong as a primary school, but was also used as a church for three Sundays a month. Campbell Slimon, who went to this school, told me about the life in that remote place of education. He recalled that before Rebecca McLean had arrived as head teacher in 1935, there were about twenty children attending. Then in the early years of the war the school roll increased by another ten, who were evacuees. Apparently, during the 1930s the children still wrote on slates; both boys and girls had to learn how to knit socks, and cut-up newspapers were used in the outside toilets! Some children had to walk as much as three miles each day, with their 'piece' for lunch, in order to reach the school.

Strict discipline was observed at the Glentruim School, the day beginning with the children being lined up outside the building, girls to the front and the boys to the back. They would then have to mark time, marching on the spot in a regimented fashion. Indeed the strict regime did not slacken from lesson to lesson, with the belt dominating the classroom.

Campbell said that the high ceilings and large windows made the school rooms cold, the only source of heat being a Courtier coke stove, which required a lot of coaxing to work properly. The high wooden ceiling was ingeniously used by the children as a dartboard, the darts being their fountain pens. When any pranks were noticed, there was punishment, and there was one lesson a certain pupil would never forget. He was dangled thirty-five feet over the Falls of Truim, by his braces! It was the schoolmistress's husband himself who dealt with this culprit.

The Falls of Truim, a short walk from the old schoolhouse, was a favourite place of mine for fishing early in the morning, before anyone in our household stirred. This river features in a book by John Hall called *Fishing a Highland Stream*, which tells of its excellent trout fishing. I had been taught to fish and to tie flies by our ghillie, Peter MacDonald. Fly-fishing was to be encouraged and spinners were out of the question! There were many fishing-rods for me to choose from in Glentruim, but I was proud to have been given my very own rod, which was light and manageable, by Euan one Christmas. I did not always catch a fish, in my limited time, but I enjoyed fishing immensely.

We never frowned upon those who were seen fishing for the pot or indeed shooting for the pot; we turned a blind eye to them. When a blue van came over from Glasgow early one morning, however, this was a different kettle o' fish! Large quantities of salmon were taken to sell on the black market. All of us in the valley were very angry when cyanide, used by these poachers in the Truim, killed every fish in the river. Cyanide drops to the bottom of the water, after depleting it of oxygen. Without oxygen the fish die, float to the surface and can then be hooked from the banks. This is an easy way for poachers to catch fish in great numbers, but it takes years for rivers to recover from such pollution.

A more amusing incident regarding theft was that of wood. Very early one morning, when I went down to the Falls of Truim in the hope of catching a salmon, I saw, stacked at the far side of the fence, a great pile of wood. It was laboriously stacked in

147

lengths, ready to be surreptitiously uplifted. The salmon fishing was abandoned; I returned home and hitched the trailer to the Land Rover and then brought the timber back to Glentruim. That saved one of the tiresome routine weekend jobs lined up for Euan. He found our wood stock well-replenished after this incident. I felt pleased with my morning's work; the salmon would have been happy to wait!

It was easy for me to keep an eye on the estate, because I was up and down the back road, ferrying children to school, checking on holiday cottages, and on more pleasurable occasions exercising the Garrons or walking the dogs. Poachers soon got to know that I did not miss a trick. Those who took their lurchers out after roe deer and left their trophy hidden, planning to pick it up when night fell, would find it gone on their return. Those who took the odd fish were given a free fishing permit in exchange for handing in every second catch to the estate. I knew we did not get every second fish, but at least we received some that we otherwise would not have had.

Poachers seemed to be worshipped by some locals: they were usually clever, witty and had daring stories to tell. By trying to outwit the landowners, they were regarded as the legendary Robin Hoods – taking from the rich and giving to the poor. But as those days had gone, now it was their personal pockets that they were lining and it was nothing to be proud of.

# 18

# *Manfred*

MANFRED first came to Glentruim through a sporting agent in Germany. By then we were making use of every single resource on the estate to bring in income. This German agent was a large, forceful man, a bit of a bully, who knew when he was on to a bargain and benefited from his intuitions. We were sent small shooting parties by this agent, but although there seemed to be a promise of good money for us, with our scant income, we soon found out that we were the losers in this deal. He would send us hunter after hunter to board, and the work involved was immeasurable. Some were nice enough but then, as always, the few spoilt it for the rest. There were turbulent days when I found myself ordered around in my own home. The ladies who accompanied their husbands would come in the most inappropriate attire and consequently froze to death in the large rambling mansion, which lacked full central heating. There were demands for more heaters in the rooms, more wood for the fires and above all, attention from me. The climax came one evening when Euan returned home from work and found me in tears from sheer exhaustion, running after the whims of these paying guests. Euan made them pack their bags, gave them their money back and told them to leave instantly.

Manfred, the head teacher of a large school in Medebach, in Germany, had perfect English and perfect manners. He first came to us through the aforementioned agent. After a dram one evening, we discussed the deal we had embarked on with the agent and Manfred, being appalled by our cut, immediately offered to be our sole agent in Germany. It was the beginning of a long and harmonious partnership.

It was not difficult to end the contract with the original German agent. This action was precipitated by an error made by our bank, which had credited our account with £1,000, deposited through our agent's bank. We had told them that it was a mistake and that it must have been 1,000 deutschmarks. 'Our bank never makes mistakes,' was the curt reply. So we sat on that money until the agent arrived at our door demanding his dues! We gave him his money and that was the last time we saw or heard of this domineering man.

Manfred came to stay many times during each year, sometimes to shoot and sometimes just to be with us. He was very good company and a fine shot. He fitted in with our daily lives and helped out with even the most menial of jobs. I remember when the wildcats first became a protected species; Manfred was aware of their destructive nature, but also aware of the laws of the country. He had been rough shooting during the early hours of the day, and had stumbled on a litter of four wildcat kittens. He knew that the mother would have had scent of him and therefore might not go back to her young. Later in the day he returned to the place to find that indeed she had abandoned them. We decided to give the kittens to the Wildlife Park in Kingussie. They were fierce creatures, young as they were; gloves were essential as they spat and clawed at us in the corner of the kitchen. Manfred had placed them there to be uplifted later that day by the warden of the Wildlife Park.

Manfred had an experience on Glentruim, when out stalking, that he told me he would never forget as long as he lived, and I relate his tale. He went off hunting one day, with the aim of stalking the top part of Glentruim hills. At the foot, before he started the climb, he stopped to decide which route he would take. Slowly and carefully he focused the lenses of his binoculars, spying from spot to spot on the sunny hillsides of Glentruim, where he knew from experience that the stags liked to rest during the day. While going along the back road he halted again and again to peer through the binoculars. When he reached the Crooked Bridge, situated halfway along the back road, his eyes fixed on a single stag, lying on a prominent rock balcony, which allowed him to watch the slope on both sides. If anything moved, the stag would be on his legs in a second to warn his fellow creatures, who were resting out of sight, relying on their attentive guard. Manfred said that he wondered whether he should try to get close to them, but after studying the possibilities, he realised that there was no cover between the birch trees and the stag. He made his way to a hollow, which led to a little plateau, between two hills. He knew that the stags used this hollow as a habitual path up from the Spey Valley, where they fed overnight. Often they lingered in the hollow before going to rest in a sheltered place on the other side of the hills. There was a deep brook in this hollow, which meant getting damp and wet if crawling in the surrounding terrain. Manfred knew that if he did not mind the water running into his boots and sometimes into his collar, then he could easily manoeuvre himself across. He did make this journey, slowly and quietly crawling, keeping his binoculars and rifle high and dry. Every so often he rose to peer over the bog in order to catch a glimpse of the stag. There was no stag to be seen at that moment, but he did catch sight of a golden eagle, with far-spread wings, only a few feet above the ground and about thirty yards away. Manfred lifted his head to watch the hovering eagle. Then down it swooped, trying to snatch a baby roe deer which was jumping about happily, oblivious of the danger, while its mother defended it courageously, with her life in peril. The mother kicked out with her hind legs to protect her young, while beating at the bird with her front legs. The eagle rose again only to swoop down once more on its prey, while its mother watched intensely. The next dive came, the eagle's claws aiming at this young roe deer. With her own body, the mother defended her baby once again. Feathers were torn from the breast of the eagle by the force of the doe's front legs. Eventually the eagle fell to the ground, exhausted, its wings hanging limply.

Manfred had gone out that morning for the trophy of a stag, instead of which, he told me, he had captured a trophy for his memory bank. Although he could not hang it on the wall, it would remain with him always, in his memories of Glentruim.

One October evening Euan and Manfred sat by the fire talking, as they often did for hours, and their topic was dreams. Euan had told Manfred how much our dreams were part of our lives and that we always have dreams when we sleep, but mostly do not remember them. As a psychologist, Euan had researched widely in this field.

Pipe in hand, whisky glass in the other, Euan chatted away to Manfred. 'Sometimes we even meet people in our dreams who we have never met before and they meet us in their dream at the same time.' Manfred was doubtful, but Euan assured him that it happens.

'In my early rock-climbing days, when I was a young man,' Euan was saying, 'I went to Glencoe for the weekend. A steep wall I had never climbed before was my aim. In brilliant weather, I reached the point from which I wished to start the next morning. As I sat in front of my little tent, the rays of the sinking sun warmed me during my simple meal, while the evening shadows gave the mountains of Glencoe, on the other side of the valley, that gloomy atmosphere, which made me think of one of the most dreadful happenings in Scottish history. In my mind's eye I watched the cowardly murder of the MacDonalds of Glencoe while they slept. Quickly the sun set and the shadows crept up to my tent, making me shudder in the suddenly chilly air, and, with a last look at my wall, I lay down and fell asleep almost immediately. In the middle of the night I woke up from a dream that stayed

152

clearly with me. I had met this most beautiful girl. From the dream I knew that she lived in the village further down the valley. But I had never been there before. I could hardly wait for the morning to come. With first light, instead of starting the climb as I intended, I hastily packed all my equipment into my knapsack and wandered down to the village from my dream. I arrived in time for breakfast in the old pub. The breakfast was served by the girl I had seen in my dream. She stared at me in utter surprise when she saw me. I could tell that she too had had this same dream, in which we had both met that previous night. I never saw her again.'

Euan had also told me of this dream, many years before, and I had no idea that he had ever mentioned it to anyone else other than me.

Manfred and his family became great friends, even sharing holidays with us. He saw both our children grow up, and it was he who made the little wooden tuckbox for Lachlan, when he was so distressed at leaving home and going back to school.

Euan and Manfred had great respect for each other, both having a love of words. They would relate proverbs through the evenings and into the early hours of the following day, comparing the similarities between one country and the other. There were political discussions as well as exchanges of a great many shooting stories.

Manfred told me of the most moving story that he had ever heard, late one night with Euan. There was a strong wind blowing around the building, making the windows rattle, and the heavy rain was pouring down, causing a crackling in the open fire. Amber-coloured whisky circled slowly in the glasses, which they both turned in their hands. Relaxing comfortably back in the old armchairs, their feet outstretched, close to the warming fire, Euan started the conversation.

'I love these sounds at night. They give me the feeling of having a home that can't be shaken by anything,' Euan said to Manfred after a long pause of mutual silence.

'Do you know that feeling of coming home in such weather after a day out, smelling the smoke of a wood fire, being pressed down by the rain, with the promise of warmth and a welcome inside?' Euan asked, sipping from his glass. 'It is one of the best feelings on earth.'

Listening to the wind's wild melody, they sank more deeply into the armchairs; their feet stretching closer to the fire and, after a period of quiet, Euan suddenly asked Manfred if he was happy with his life as it was. The question came as a surprise to Manfred, so he took time before his answer came to him.

'To be happy means to be in heaven – this earth and life, as it is, is not heaven. But there have been many happy moments in my life, and I accept life gladly as it is. It is not heaven. I have four healthy and wonderful children. What more can I expect?'

'You are so right,' replied Euan. 'To have children is the main thing. To know that the stream of blood is flowing on, to have children means that one has not lived in vain. Children are the real print we leave, when we have to go.'

The smoke rose from Euan's pipe and then the whisky glass went to his lips, as they talked of their ups and downs and of their family lives. The expression on Euan's face portrayed his thoughts, far back in the past, the past which imposed such obligations on him.

'You cannot break the line of a thousand years of family history.' This was one of Euan's many sayings. The present sharply returned to Euan's bearded face and with a smile he murmured, 'Nevertheless, I am a very lucky man,' and seeing the unasked question in Manfred's face he continued, 'I could show you a picture of Sandra and you would know that I am one of the very few lucky men who met an angel on earth.'

Manfred then told me that, with the happiest expression that he had ever watched on Euan's face, he had added, 'And the angel stayed with me.'

## Manfred

'Could you think of a more wonderful declaration of love?' Manfred asked me years later, when life was a struggle, Euan fighting for the survival of Glentruim and I embarking on venture after venture to make ends meet.

# 19

# *Miss Marble*

ISABELLA McIntosh Melville, the great-granddaughter of A. H. McIntosh, the renowned furniture manufacturer in Kirkcaldy, was known to us as Tibbie. She was a friend of my parents so I had known her since I was seven years old. Tibbie had lived in Murthly until she was widowed, and then moved to London, where she worked for the BBC. She then returned to Scotland, becoming the editor of the *Glasgow Illustrated*, the Scottish society magazine published by the Tatler Group. Whilst married and living in Murthly, her husband Pat was a well-known face on the vintage car racing circuit and had competed in many events at Silverstone. As a result Tibbie was familiar with driving many different makes of cars – ranging from a Triumph Herald to the first Porsche in Scotland. With such experience she was the ideal person to fill the breach when we required a chauffeuse to pick up a party of Germans who were arriving for two weeks' holiday.

Since her husband's demise Tibbie has spent every Christmas with us at Glentruim. Even when in London she strove to visit us at least once a year. The party of Germans had asked if we could meet them at Inverness Airport. The day before, I checked with the airport, but found no planes were due to come in around what they had given as their expected time of arrival. Telephoning Germany, I discovered that they were arriving in their own aeroplane and that the time given was a rough guide, dependent on flight control.

Three days before this visit, it had been necessary to remove a lump which was attached to a muscle in my leg and so, because of the booking, I had asked if I could have the surgery carried out with a local anaesthetic. This was a bad idea because the operation, which was undertaken by a young Australian doctor, proved to be more difficult than expected. I was sent home the same day with strong analgesics and a walking-stick. I was glad that we had made the decision to house all paying guests in the self-catering cottages. This made my workload much lighter.

After Tibbie had arrived, I handed her the keys of the Land Rover with a cautionary reminder that the reverse gears did not work. I also asked her to take the guests shopping before returning to Glentruim so that they could stock up with provisions.

It was a hot spring day and my peahens were laying eggs in hidey-holes around the grounds. Normally, I would try to watch them to see where their nests were before foxes and wildcats could take both peahen and the eggs beneath her. I followed one peahen from a safe distance behind, with stick in hand, in considerable pain from the stitches and bruising in my leg. The peahen crossed the top terrace, stopping occasionally to glance behind her, suspecting that she was being watched. The nest was likely to be very close at hand, but she took me on a round-about route before dashing into the undergrowth near the woods, below the terraced lawns. Having hobbled this distance, I could not see her because she was lying low and still. Sitting in the scooped-out nest in the ground, this bird made easy prey for its predators and I knew that I would have to make another attempt later, in order to retrieve the eggs and put them under the hatching light.

If the peahen and eggs were not taken by wildlife, the newly-hatched chicks only needed one downpour of rain to be soaked, after which they would perish. They were also very vulnerable until they got on their feet and were then later assisted onto a branch by their mother. When they were tiny, the mother would place them on her back and would try to keep them safe, but they were always in danger until they were older and stronger.

I loved my peafowl and I had about ten in all. But they were not so liked by the rest of the family, who found them noisy. However, the children enjoyed collecting the pretty feathers shed by the males. The number of rows of eyes on these tail feathers indicates the bird's age, one row being for each year. There was an ancient superstition which maintained that these eyes belonged to the devil, and this is why it is deemed unlucky to bring the feathers into the house. The children only brought them in once, and that was into the kitchen. Soon after the feathers had been taken into the room, a cupboard fell off the wall, breaking every dish that was inside and cracking the worktop surface. A coincidence perhaps, but that was the last time a peacock's feather crossed the threshold!

The peacocks were disliked intensely by visitors due to their habit of sitting on the bonnets of their expensive cars, to preen themselves in the windscreen or wing-mirrors. They were also a nuisance when they made themselves at home in the conservatory. The worst escapade of an old peacock was to crash through the bathroom skylight in the main guest suite; he was probably more shocked than the person in the bath!

I found the peafowl very biddable, but then I was the one who fed them. They were so tame that I could hold a peanut, in its shell, between my teeth and they would gently take it from me. They would even allow me to stroke the soft white feathers below their wings. I recall the day I bought the first four, two hens and two cocks. We were on holiday on the West Coast and they were for sale in Inverewe Gardens. I could not resist them.

Tibbie had a difficult return journey in the Land Rover: she did not speak German and the four men had very little English. She could not make them understand that they had to stop for provisions. They arrived back at Glentruim in a fluster. They kept referring to Tibbie as 'Miss Marble', a mixture of Melville

158

and Miss Marple! They were under the impression that they were staying with us, not in a holiday cottage. My heart sank; the thought of looking after a party of men, with my leg being so painful, was too much for me. We made a compromise, they stayed in the cottage and came to us for dinner every second night.

On the Sunday there was no shooting, so the men suggested that they should show 'Miss Marble' Scotland by air. She was to have a trip with them in the morning and our family was invited for the afternoon. The children were very excited. We met at Inverness airport to find that Tibbie had experienced a wonderful morning.

It was our turn and we clambered into the Cessna. We were to be shown the whole of Glentruim estate. As we swooped down and round, the stitches in my leg were pulled against gravity. The pilot was so excited about seeing Glentruim at all angles that I had to shut my eyes for fear of crashing. The children's screams were interpreted by the pilot as squeals of delight, but in fact they too were utterly terrified. The more the children screamed, the more daring the pilot became. Catriona said years later that this flight had put her off flying in small planes for ever! Nearing the end of this air tour of Glentruim estate, Euan, who had flown aircraft before, was given the controls. This further turned my stomach and we landed just in time for me to reach the nearest ladies' room!

Tibbie rocked our children as babies, bounced them on her knee when toddlers, and played on the floor with them when they were older. They adored her and she was like a second granny to them. Christmas was a magical time at Glentruim, especially if there was snow. We always kept to all the traditions, which Euan held dear; our routine never changed.

We felled our own Christmas tree from the woods off the avenue, and it would be about twelve feet high. The whole family used to go off with the trailer; then followed a ritual to choose the right tree, after which time would be spent contemplating the felling. Back at Glentruim, the tree would stand at the bottom of the well of the front staircase, almost reaching the ceiling of the landing above. The rest of the day was spent decorating it.

In the basement was a cupboard in which were stored old tins of decorations going back generations. These were toffee and biscuit tins, all with pictures on the top advertising their wares. Inside we would keep candle-holders, delicate peacocks with fanned tails made of threads of nylon, straw and papier-mâché figurines, wooden animals and lots of coloured balls of all shapes and sizes. They were very fragile, but even the damaged ones went on the tree.

Electricity was not supplied to Glentruim until the early 1960s, so until then the little candles were lit in their holders on the Christmas tree. Although we carried on the tradition of hosting a children's party, the children who came to us were from the village rather than from the estate, as in the days of Aunt Katie. In Katie's time there would be about ten youngsters. There would be the gardeners', the keepers', the shepherds' and the farmers' children. They would all be from houses on the estate, which included a household that lived in a little wooden house down by the Truim Bridge. The wooden house was made of railway sleepers but in later years it was burnt down, never to be built again. Fortunately nobody was hurt in the fire.

Campbell Slimon, one of these farmers' children, now with children and grandchildren of his own, told me that he remembered the lit candles on the Christmas tree and was intrigued when they were extinguished by a long candle snuffer. There would be a Santa Clause there, the only one the children would come across during the festive period. It would in fact be the only party for them in the area. The Christmas crackers on the tea-table were the gifts at the party. Campbell mimicked a friend of Katie's shouting in a shrill voice after her, when she left the table, while children waited patiently to pull the crackers, 'Katie, you've forgotten the crackers!' It was a good impersonation.

There was one Christmas when Euan was not well enough to go for the Christmas tree. Catriona must have been about twelve and Lachlan nine years old. Catriona had by then learnt to drive and, with the aid of cushions, managed the Land Rover adequately around our private land. So the two children went, with the trailer, in search of the Christmas tree. Catriona amused us when she told us of their adventure that day. They had taken a bow-saw and, having chosen their tree, got to work. Their concentration was so extreme that they both had eyes tightly shut. Catriona could not understand why the saw was so stiff until she opened her eyes and saw Lachlan pulling against her. Determination eventually took them home with success; the tree was magnificent and they both felt very proud that Christmas.

A day or two before Christmas Eve, the children from Laggan School used to come for the festive party. The dining-room table was covered with home-made cakes, biscuits, sandwiches, jellies and of course, crackers. After the tea party my father, who was a member of the Magic Circle, was the conjurer. I remember a trick which involved my father drinking a glass of beer and then the glass mysteriously filled up again. A little boy of about four, said, 'That's just like my father, he does that every night!' Then there were children's games and finally all would go home with balloons and token presents.

My parents came every Christmas and there was sure to be some sort of mishap either on the journey north or on the return. If snow lay thick on the ground, the main roads were treacherous and Drumochter Pass would be closed. They nearly always made it through Drumochter to get to us, but once or twice we had to go to the rescue. My father once mistook a layby for the main road and, speeding in, found himself over the verge and in a field.

My mother was not at all happy when we pulled them out. Medicinal drinking started early that Christmas!

I thought that Christmas should be special for everyone and that nobody should have to spend this time of the year alone. During the early years at Glentruim I had learnt that John Sparrow, the son of one of my mother's old boyfriends, had been spending many a Christmas alone. So he too soon became part of our regular Christmas guests.

Catriona must have been as passionate about Christmas as I was. There was one afternoon just before Christmas when I had left the children with a young girl in the house and had gone into the village for shopping. It was getting dark on my way home, but there, hovering above the Truim at the bridge I saw what I thought was an unidentified flying object. I immediately went up the drive to fetch the children to show them this extraordinary light. On the way back down to the bridge I told them what I had seen, but, when we got there it had gone. As we drove home Catriona looked very pensive, then she said, 'Mummy, if a lady comes to our door tonight and is sitting on a donkey, will you let her in?' I was amused to see how serious she was. It being so close to Christmas she must have thought that I had seen the Star of Bethlehem! I did call the police later to notify them of what I thought I had seen. They duly came with their note pads and jotted down my recollections for their records of UFO sightings. I was not the only person who had experienced this light that night. I was told by the police that they had already been notified of this alleged sighting by the manager of the Dalwhinnie Distillery!

Christmas is an exhausting time for young mothers, with so much to remember to do and so much preparation. The number of toys that had to be constructed on Christmas Eve was exasperating. Because instructions were certainly not made for children, we adults could spend hours, late that night, trying to put minute pegs in 'Cindy's Caravan' or piece together 'Action

Man's helicopter'. That was before wrapping other gifts for stocking-fillers.

The start of Christmas Day was as early as the children woke, though as they got older it got a little later. After opening their stockings the busy day would begin. Everyone in the house would have a stocking, even the adults. I would be first down to light the fires and to make preparations for the Christmas dinner before tackling breakfast. The lights were reflected on the polished floor in the hall and Christmas carols set the scene for the day. Under the tree, presents were piled high and stretched out into the middle of the floor. No presents were opened until everyone had come downstairs and had breakfast. The ritual of opening presents was accompanied by a warming drink, of whisky and Crabbies Green Ginger for the adults – a whisky Mac.

I would sit with pencil and paper, marking down each present and who had given what to whom, so that thank-you letters could be sent immediately after Christmas was over. The children ripped open their presents in excitement and there was paper littered everywhere. As fast as Tibbie put the paper in a black bag there would be more to pick up.

We always had a snack lunch of homemade soup and Christmas cake as the children, their faces flushed with excitement, sat mesmerised by their presents. Before the feast of the late afternoon, everyone was obliged to go for a walk up the torr and then on our return we would all get dressed for the Christmas dinner.

On Boxing Day, presents were enjoyed and the children played with their own gifts. Lachlan's main present frequently had a part missing, no batteries, or was just too difficult for him to operate. I never seemed to get it quite right. Lachlan had to be very patient when his father and grandfather played endlessly with his most exciting toy. His little voice would chirp, 'Can I have a turn now?' 'In a minute,' came the answer as his elders were engrossed in play. Hardly a minute would pass before Lachlan repeated his request.

We are not alone in our magic memories of Christmas at Glentruim. Today I still meet children from those earlier times, now grown-up and with children of their own at Laggan School, remarking on those wonderful Christmas parties at Glentruim.

# 20

# *The Caravan Park*

IN the early 1970s caravan parks were booming. During the summer the narrow roads in Scotland were packed with holiday-makers towing their caravans from one park to the other, much to the frustration of other drivers. Having generated substantial capital through selling timber, our intention was either to build chalets or to construct a caravan park, which might eventually give us a profitable business. We decided to build a caravan park in the bottom fields, on the old site of the battle of Invernahavon. We named it 'Invernahavon Caravan Park'.

Although it was an exciting prospect for us, this new enterprise became fraught with difficulties from beginning to end. We hired an architect from Pitlochry, who drew up detailed plans. How-ever, although the construction firm was adamant that the work had been carried out according to the specifications, to us there seemed to be defects. The main problem was the parking area, which, in our opinion, was not level. This caused nearly two years of dispute between us and the firm in question, ending in a very unpleasant court case, to our disadvantage. We then had the added burden of enormous costs, which we could ill afford. Euan became exceedingly anxious and the publicity given to this case made him very depressed. It was imperative that the caravan park should succeed, but, when the price of petrol rose during the following years, it was apparent that this business would never begin to cover our increasing debts.

The morning after the judgement of the court case we really hit the headlines. I got up early to go into the village to buy the newspapers before the shop became busy. The tabloids were full of our troubles, with a picture of Euan on the front, the caption 'Clan Chieftain Loses Court Case' in large bold letters. It was also mentioned on the local television news: we could not hide from it. Euan lay low, but I had promised to play my clarsach at a ceilidh in Newtonmore village hall that evening, and I knew that if I did not appear it would be even more difficult to show my face later.

I had asked my mother to come to stay, and also to accompany me to the ceilidh. Encouraging though it was to have her support, all the same there was a sinking feeling in my stomach as I carried my clarsach onto the stage. Several weeks prior to this evening, I had transposed Cavatina, the theme-music from the *Deer Hunter*, on to the clarsach for Euan, who loved this tune, and it was this that I played first in front of a packed hall. My hands trembled as my fingers pulled each string; the audience listened so intently that you could have heard a pin drop. I drifted with the music, thinking of Euan stalking the deer on the hills of Glentruim. This was what I associated with the tune, not the atrocities shown in the film for which the tune was composed. Applause from those in front of me below the stage lifted my low spirits. At the interval a great many people came to speak to me, their faces smiling with encouragement. Their words were unnecessary, however, because I knew then that inwardly they supported me just as they had earlier, despite our public insult. I was glad that I had had the courage to play, conquering my fear of ridicule because of the court case, and I was determined to block out the previous two years of tension.

We carried on running the caravan park, employing a couple to maintain it each summer season. Our handyman and his wife, whom we had taken on years before, were also available for short periods in the quieter months, to undertake essential work in the park. With its shop to run and the shower blocks to clean, as well as the booking-in of caravans, there was always plenty to do. The site was divided into bays, between each of which there were areas of grass. These Euan usually cut with gang-mowers.

Because Euan was confined to his bed the day the gang-mowers were to be picked up from Aberdeen, I had to go in his place. It must have been one of the trickiest journeys I ever had to make with Land Rover and trailer, through Tomintoul and by various back roads over the hills, regardless of blizzard conditions. After such a long journey with a trailer, needless to say I was very relieved to return home.

Margaret Morrison first came to help me with the house and the children during her university holidays. At the time, she was studying law at Dundee and Dean, her long standing-boyfriend, was a medical student at Edinburgh. After a couple of years Dean joined Margaret at Glentruim and together they ran the caravan park for us each summer until they qualified and then eventually married. We all thought that Margaret and Dean were lovely together. Margaret was petite, with a fine-featured face, large brown eyes and short, thick, white hair, which made a startling contrast to such a young face. Dean, though not much taller than her, was of athletic build. Margaret laughed when I showed her the duties that went with the caravan park. 'And a tickly under there,' I would say, with the brush down the U-bends in the toilet blocks, trying to make her work more fun, trying to cover my embarrassment that she would have to do such cleaning.

The sheep had a habit of escaping out of their fields and grazing through the park, which meant we would all be down there herding them out. Euan was the best at this. When one of the visitors asked Dean, who was working in the shop, the best way to get rid of the sheep at his caravan door, Dean described Euan's method as follows: 'Well,' he said, as he came from the other side of the serving-counter, in his T-shirt and scanty white shorts, 'This is what the Laird does.' But as he bent up and down, raising outstretched arms above his head, shouting 'Whoosh!', he broke wind. Margaret, who witnessed this scene, felt as if she might explode. She managed to control herself before she crumpled into laughter, as the visitor replied, straight-faced, when he walked out of the shop, 'OK, sir'. He licked his right index finger, held it high in the air and added, 'I suppose it depends on which way the wind blows!'

The bullocks were not very popular when they wandered through the park, and there was one very large white bull that was a frequent passer-by. If I was assisting Margaret on a busy day in the toilet-blocks and the bull came in view, there would be a mad dash to the shop to telephone Euan. If available, he would come down to the caravan park with a stick and no fear. Margaret and I both looked aghast at one another one afternoon when we saw the white bull rub himself against one of the caravans. Frightened faces peered through the window, as the caravan rocked to and fro. When the bull had finished, he nonchalantly ambled to the next caravan. We could see two elderly people sitting at their picnic table on the grass, at the far side of this caravan. As the bull approached their table they fled inside as fast as their old legs could take them.

After the main season ended for the park, there would be nobody living in the warden's caravan. If the odd tent or caravan came in, our handyman, his wife or I would collect the fees in the evening. On one occasion a solitary tent had been pitched near the back fence, but every time I went to check it, there was no vehicle or sign of occupants. For a week I went down in the evenings at different times to see if I could catch the owners. Then I tried early in the mornings, but still without success. Getting suspicious, I thought that I would have a look inside the tent; it was full of pieces of silverware. I had read in the news-papers of burglaries up and down the valley, even as far as Fort William, all of which had occurred at country houses. I went back to Glentruim, alerted the police and returned to the caravan park to find three young men throwing tent and loot into their car. However, as they took off, the police were not far behind them and the culprits were caught just before they reached Drumochter Pass.

At times, on the way down to the caravan park early in the day, I would come across a capercailzie. Indeed there were quite a few of these magnificent birds on the Glentruim estate. The oldest male marked his territory by strutting slowly up and down the front avenue each morning. He knew me, since I frequently passed by him and I had the privilege of getting quite close. One day I found him ill and lying at the side of the drive. I wrapped his heavy body in a blanket and took him to Kennel Cottage. There I lay him on straw in the empty kennels which were attached to the cottage. Having spoken to the local vet on the telephone, it was decided that nothing could be done. The vet also said that I had taken a risk handling a capercailzie; one swipe from this bird's massive wings could have caused me severe damage! When he died we had him preserved by a taxidermist, and he now remains in the hall at Glentruim. A younger male capercailzie immediately took his place and quickly marked his inherited territory. I did also see these birds walking up and down the flat part of the roof at Glentruim, when I was bringing in washing one night. As Euan was quick to remark, their presence could explain some of the ghostly footsteps heard at night!

All the strangeness of Glentruim was heightened for Margaret when I took her and Dean to a function in Newtonmore. This was to raise money for Newtonmore Primary School, the main attraction being Swein Macdonald, the Brahan Seer. There had always been a strong tradition of the second sight (Da Shealladh) in the Highlands, and the Brahan Seer was endowed with this gift. This person succeeded Kenneth Mackenzie, the former Brahan Seer and a legendary figure, who was considered to be a prophet second only to Nostradamus. Such seers had an important role in Celtic society. Swein, from the Black Isle, was the new Brahan Seer of the time, a big, impressive man with white hair and a bushy white beard. He told stories and then focused on the audience.

That evening Swein pinpointed certain people, first telling them of things in their past, which he could not have known, and then foretold their future. There was a tourist in the audience, sitting at the back. She was a rather odd person, who stood up and aggressively tackled Swein about his predictions. We were all astounded by her audacious attitude. Swein made no answer, merely looking her straight in the eye from the other side of the hall until she relented. After a few mumbles, she retracted her words and sat down.

Swein was a good friend of Donald MacDonald, the head-master of Newtonmore Primary School, with whom he and his wife were staying the night. I was invited to go back for a drink after the performance, lingering at least an hour, while the invited visitors listened to stories of second sight, hauntings, and a fanciful tale of three horsemen riding through Swein's bedroom. This was embellished by his wife, Isobel, who chipped in, emphasising bizarre recollections and adding comments, which made his tales all the more fantastic but nevertheless convincing. These stories were about real people, folk not very far away, in Easter Ross, the Black Isle and all over Inverness-shire!

Much later in the year Swein came to Glentruim to meet Euan. As we sat at the kitchen table, he told us how he had fallen in love with a young girl in a dream and had planned to marry her. He added that he had no idea that this would actually happen in his life. We found out years later that his dream had indeed come true. Because Euan could not understand how 'The Brahan Seer' could not foresee his own future, to him Swein's credibility was immediately flawed.

There was devastation in the caravan park in 1979. We were attending local Highland Games at Dalhully Estate, which at that time was owned by Alex Herbage, and had been invited there for lunch before the event. Alex was so extremely large that he had to have a seat especially made for him in his Range Rover. His wife's stature was to the opposite extreme, for she was small and slender. None of us really knew what their line of business was, but we knew that he had bodyguards and was often taken off to meetings in his helicopter.

While we chatted to Alex and his wife before lunch, our children disappeared. I was mortified to hear later that they had snooped in our hosts' bedroom to see if the local gossip was correct. It was indeed: there were sixteen reinforced legs on the extra-large king-sized bed!

After a very good meal and wine, we walked a short distance to the gamesfield. Alex was driven at a slow pace in his Range Rover and we all followed behind on foot, rather like a funeral cortège. When Euan and I were asked to join Alex and his wife on the platform, I sat beside him, with Euan on the other side of his wife, as we watched the games. Afternoon tea came on silver platters, in the form of large quantities of sandwiches and cakes. I had no room for more food after such an ample lunch, but Alex, however, tucked in; when all the cakes and sandwiches were finished he then started eating the paper napkins!

Towards the end of the games the skies suddenly darkened. Above the furthest hill and veering towards us, we all saw the vortex-shaped outline of a tornado. There was urgency in our haste to get to our transport and as we drove home we could see the tornado getting closer and closer. We got indoors just in time before it struck. It blew right through the conservatory, taking with it two sides. Splinters of glass were scattered across the drive, uprooted trees were hurled across the torr, and the avenue was strewn with branches. It was terrifying.

Most of the destruction was in the caravan park. The toilet blocks had been turned upside down and literally inside out. Toilets, shower-units and basins lay shattered on the ground all around the park. There were no touring caravans in at the time, only those that were sited there all year round. These caravans had been pinned to the ground for the winter, but the pins had been useless against such a powerful storm; they too had been upturned and wrecked. This was just another story in the accumulation of unfortunate events which plagued our caravan site. Fortunate visitors who had enjoyed a holiday there without any mishap would have been surprised to know how many unusual and devastating disruptions had occurred over the years.

# 21

# *The Portraits*

WHEN paying guests came to stay, it often happened that they ended up becoming our friends. Our culture and our traditions enthralled them. In Scotland many people know their heritage and family lines and some, such as our Glentruim family, can trace their families back for centuries. This was what most intrigued our visitors. They would walk into our museum in the house and look at our family tree, which dates back to the eleventh century. We had people from America just dropping in saying, 'We think we are related to you!' I would take them into the museum and let them study the family tree and work it out for themselves.

Euan was much better than I with the history of Glentruim, and the house museum was packed with objects of historic interest, pictures and weapons. Euan had arranged this room, which was as good as any public museum you could care to visit. In it there were three large glass display-cabinets, which Euan had bought at a sale room in Inverness. They had come from a draper's shop and on the top front edge of each there was a brass ruler, in inches, embedded in the glass. Pictures of Glentruim, before and after the conservatory and the dining-room were added, hung on the walls, along with old family black and white photographs. These were intermingled with spears brought back from India by ancestors, along with other objects such as primitive snowshoes, which looked like large tennis rackets, with their ties hanging down. The ties would have been secured around the ankle.

Tattered marriage contracts lay open in the cabinets, under glass on the shelves, showing us each dowry promised on the occasion of marriage into the family of Glentruim. There were also miniatures of members of the family with names and dates written in ink on small pieces of brown paper beside them; a small pistol from the Forty-Five, belonging to the Glentruim family; also a silver cross from the Forty-Five and many other artefacts. The cross was a good three inches in breadth, two inches in width, with green jade set in the stems. I later commandeered it for myself, deciding that it should be worn and not displayed!

There were portraits in Glentruim of past Macphersons and of their wives. Latterly one was painted of Euan, but for a long time there was none of me or of the children. We planned to put this right by commissioning the Honourable Mrs Honor Earl to draw myself, Catriona and Lachlan, in pastel. This was in 1976, when I was thirty, Catriona was five and Lachlan was two. We had already been shown striking drawings of the Haywood children which Honor had done and had been very impressed by her talent.

Honor was the niece of the late Somerset Maugham and was in her seventies when she came to draw for us. It was autumn and she had come straight from the Castle of May, where she had been working on pastel drawings for the Queen Mother. Not having much help in the house at this time, I was anxious because Honor had just stayed with a distinguished lady with a household of servants. She set up her easel in her bedroom, which faced north-east, giving her the best light on her canvas. She was a small, precise lady with no airs and graces and I knew that we would get on fine together during the long hours ahead of us.

I was the first to be drawn. I was asked to wear a ballgown and to be ready the next morning as soon as she had taken breakfast in her room. I duly sat for hours, with a fixed expression on my face, lips slightly parted, and was asked to look towards Honor's left shoulder as she sat with her back to the window. Later I would be smartly snapped out of my daydreams by her midday request: 'I think we will break for lunch now.' I then had to take off my gown quickly in my bedroom, dash down the back stairs, prepare lunch and set up the dining-room, as if it had all been done behind the scenes by my servants! At lunch I had remarks such as, 'Delicious meal', and, 'Is your cook Scottish?' to which I replied, 'Oh yes, she is Scottish!' Then there was a speedy retreat up the back stairs and into my ballgown for the afternoon session.

The end result of the portrait was very pleasing, but I did ask her to alter my mouth. Honor told me that her subjects were never pleased with their mouths, because they never saw them still. I suspect she was correct!

Next it was Catriona's turn. Before Honor started this next drawing she told me that she had lost her glasses and could not possibly draw without them. I hunted everywhere, but they were not to be found. 'Never mind,' said Honor, 'They will turn up, it will be Joey.'

'Who's Joey?' I asked with curiosity.

'Oh, Joey is my poltergeist, he comes everywhere with me,' replied Honor.

'Well,' I said, 'he will have a 'field-day, because we have one too!'

Our poltergeist played games on us all the time, particularly if we had an adolescent housemaid living in. Bells would ring and I would go to the brass bells in the downstairs back corridor to find the billiard-room bell swinging, but no one in the billiard room when I went to have a look. Doors would be locked and unlocked; lights would go on and off.

I remember a night when Catriona was in the nursery and I had turned the light off in my bedroom; before going to sleep a strange thing happened. On the mantelpiece of my room there sat a bicycle torch which, all of a sudden, went on and shone in my eyes. I put on my bedside light and crossed the room to turn the bicycle light off, then went back to bed. As I felt uneasy about this, I left the side light on, but then it went off. I braved the short distance to the main light switch on the wall and flicked it on, but by this time Catriona was crying in the nursery. I was very happy to take Catriona into my bed, but when she started waving and smiling at nothing in the room, I quickly took her back to her cot. I had an adolescent girl living in at the time and therefore was not totally surprised by the tricks of a poltergeist.

There was also another extraordinary occasion when a particular maid had left the house for good, having worked for us for quite some time. I had retired to bed early in the evening, having locked all the doors, including those at the front and back. Our labrador slept between the two locked back doors. The next morning I went downstairs to find the labrador sitting in the hall, with all the doors not only unlocked but wide open! I wondered whether the poltergeist, triggered by the housemaid, had carried out its final prank for us and had then gone with her!

I was right about Honor's poltergeist having fun. We found her glasses later, exactly where she had left them on the dressing-table, and where we had certainly looked before. Then, that night, pillows were mixed from bedroom to bedroom. The pink room had yellow pillows, the yellow room had blue pillows, and the blue room had pink pillows! Both Honor and I laughed about this and wondered what was to happen next.

Catriona was fidgety when sitting for her portrait, but Honor held her attention. She drew with her right hand, and on her left was a little animated bear puppet called Winky, who sang nonsense rhymes and hit Honor on the head! I think the pastel made Catriona look older than her years, but it was enchanting. We were pleased with both. They were framed behind non-reflecting glass and we placed them in the drawing-room on either side of the gilt mirror above the fireplace. Lachlan could not sit still, because he was too young, and so his portrait had to be planned for the future.

Johnnie Bruck was one of the most talented artists I have ever met. He came from Bavaria, where he lived with his wife Bonnie and their daughter Katja. Bonnie lived up to her name, with enviable good looks. Johnnie had an impressive face and, although not particularly tall, a commanding presence. Having a square build, he suited the clothes and feathered hat which were the traditional Bavarian hunting attire.

It was in the early 1970s that Johnnie came to Glentruim to shoot: photographs, rather than game. He was a famous journalist in his own country and also took photographs to accompany his articles for sporting magazines. He said that Euan was the most distinguished-looking Highland gentleman that he had ever seen, his face being full of character. Unlike mine, he said about me, which had no lines, and to which therefore he could not do justice in a painting until I grew older, so he said! Johnnie's refusal to paint my portrait after completing that of Euan was the spur to my determination to find another artist to draw me for the Glentruim collection.

Johnnie took several photographs of Euan, in full regalia, outside the conservatory one bright day. The sun was shining in Euan's eyes, which made him frown, looking even more stern and fearsome than he really was. His deep brown eyes in the portrait followed your gaze and yes, he looked angry. But it was a skilful painting, with dark stormy skies in the background to match Euan's eyes.

We have certain black and white photographs taken by Johnnie during his stay which tell stories, including one of Euan and Bonnie. It was taken in front of Glentruim, beside our two cannons on the front lawn, Euan in Highland garb and Bonnie in a long dress. In Bonnie's hand is a dagger, which is raised above her as if ready to plunge it straight into the kilted gentle-

man before her. This scene could have been straight out of a
Shakespeare play!

Johnnie also photographed wildlife. Having developed the
films, he transformed the birds and animals in his photographs
into paintings, which he then gave to Euan. His fox painting
hung in the 'Laird's Loo' and other scenes hung in the boudoir.
One of these paintings was of Euan, clad in kilt and shirt, with
labrador and gun, walking over the Glentruim hills. He is knee-
deep in rich purple heather, the crags of Craig Dhu behind him.
It is one of those paintings which makes you imagine that you
are actually there. His drawings, however, are unique, especially
his caricatures. Every time he sent us a letter it would contain
either a drawing of game or a caricature of Euan, on the top or
at the foot of each sheet of paper. My favourite of these is of Euan
dancing the sword dance, with an exaggeratedly large head and
feathered bonnet, five arms with dagger in one hand, and four
legs. The backdrop consists of a distant view of Glentruim, a
piper and a Highland soldier standing directly behind Euan.
Under this is written, in broken English:

> 'Don't you say! Glentruim you say?'
> 'Yeah!'
> 'But that's incredible, it can't be the same Granny told
> my father about when he was still a kid!'
> 'There we are, laddie – got to be the same feller – because
> . . . in the first place he's supposed to be immortal . . . in
> the second place – in his family nobody could ever dance
> like him!'

All Johnnie's drawings were unusual, particularly the one he
headed, 'Till a' the seas gang dry and fare thee weel a while'. This
is Euan, with the roots of a tree for legs; he is again in full
Highland dress and flowing plaid, holding a glass up to his own
portrait. His own head in the portrait leans forwards, a smile on

its face, its eyes tight shut, with a long tongue lapping up the whisky from the glass! For good measure and as a token, Johnnie has added my sheltie dog in a light pencil drawing to the right of the tree roots! We now have a gallery of Johnnie's paintings and drawings.

In all the many years Johnnie came to visit us, he stayed out for hours, striding over the hills of Glentruim, shooting with his camera. When he returned to Bavaria we would receive more letters, more caricatures and more paintings. In the 1980s we were shocked by his death in a motorbike accident. He was certainly a loss to us, and a greater loss to the world of journalism and art.

# 22

# *Home Industry*

IT was like painting the Forth Rail Bridge, expense after expense, to maintain our houses, farms and land. Furthermore, repairs were continual and just when we thought they were finished, we only had to start all over again.

We shuddered at the thought that a time would come when we would have to replace the whole of the roof of the house, instead of patching it bit by bit. There was a flat, bitumen covered surface adjacent to the base of the tower which caused endless problems. Euan would get to this part of the roof through a bottom window of the tower and I would have to hold him on a length of rope until he finished each repair. There were expanses of roof-space above the bedrooms, reached through hatches in the back corridor, outside the 'Army' bedroom and in one of the bathrooms, where the insulation was of straw, a hazard in itself, as were the bees working at their honeycombs in the same area. The bees swarmed at least twice a year above the conservatory and smoke bombs were the only answer to eradicate this.

I went through life at Glentruim embarking on project after project to keep us afloat financially. My first home industry was small. It came about because of a winter activity of mine, which was to make all of our Christmas presents. The gifts varied from homemade fondant and shortbread to macramé pot-hangers, collages made from game feathers, beans and beads, to knitwear and crochet. It was a hive of industry at Glentruim during the long nights of late autumn and winter. However, I was one of those lucky people who actually enjoyed the short days, which stemmed from having to stop outside work early because of the ensuing darkness. This gave me an excuse to light the fires and cosy down for the evening. I then worked on my Christmas gifts.

Penny Weir had started her pottery business and called it Craig Dhu Pottery. She was turning out skilled pieces of pottery and exhibited at craft fairs all over Scotland. When she found out that I was working at macramé, she asked if I would join her on a stand at the Aviemore Annual Craft Trade Fair. I was delighted to accept and we had successful days together, which gave us pin-money. She made the pots which hung in my macramé baskets. Every year our favourite venue was Perth where, just before Christmas, we made lots of money. We took turns manning the stand while the other went into Perth shops to spend the daily takings on presents, thus coming home penniless but happy, our Christmas shopping completed.

Pin-money was inadequate, however, and I knew that if we were to keep Glentruim another business outlet was vital. Euan had a waistcoat that had belonged to his grandfather and it was embroidered in petit-point, very intricate, in the design of the Macpherson Hunting Tartan. It was threadbare in places and would have benefited from repair. I decided, however, to copy this waistcoat and make a new one as Euan's Christmas present. It took days to work out the design, then hours and hours of laborious work to embroider it in cross stitch. This was what gave me the idea for our next business. I started to design tapestry kits for cushions and stools, in which there were ultimately twenty-five different tartans. I had the stools made for the kits by the patients of Erskine Hospital, which is situated near Glasgow, then marketed them all over Scotland, England, France, Germany and America. Designing the charts for buyers to follow was painstaking because I had to sit at the kitchen table, with a large magnifying light and make little crosses on large graph paper. Then I would write out the instructions for each tartan design. I used Anchor wool in the packs and the director of Coates, a company in Glasgow which provided this yarn, was caught up in my enthusiasm and was more than helpful when I approached him to ask for his advice. His manageress used to say to me, 'Out of small acorns grow large trees', a remark which certainly encouraged me.

I utilised rooms in the basement of Glentruim as the centre for packing the kits and employed our handyman's wife to carry out this work. We did well, selling our kits to Scotch House, Harrods, John Lewis, as well as boutiques in Paris and National Trust shops.

I therefore soon found myself on the treadmill of trade fairs both at home and abroad. I remember, when the children were very young, setting off for Germany in an old car that used to belong to my parents, crammed so full of boxes of tartan kit samples that I could hardly see out of the rear window. I was on my way to catch the ferry in Hull to travel to Dortmund and had only got as far as Stirling when the car broke down. It was very early in the morning, I was alone on the road, and I had to walk to the nearest AA telephone box to call for help. When I returned, a lorry driver stopped and was adamant that he should assist me with the car, but my legs were shaking so much that I kept my windows shut and doors locked, saying that I would wait until the AA man arrived. The mechanic arrived shortly afterwards; he corrected the fault and I then carried on with my journey. On the other side of the Channel, driving to Dortmund proved easier than I had expected, and I arrived in good time in order to set up my stand. I was there for ten days, longing to be home from the outset. Every night I would telephone Glentruim to make sure that all was well and to give Euan an update on my progress. There was not much that I could do from so far away when I heard of all the misfortunes back home.

The first mishap during my Dortmund trip was that Catriona found my sheltie Crubie lying on the floor, producing green foam from his mouth. She alerted her father, but it was she herself who remembered that the rat poison strategically placed around the house was green. I listened to a long saga from Catriona about taking Crubie to the vet in Grantown-on-Spey, George Rafferty, who had also told Euan to bring one of our other dogs with him to the surgery. This was so that the fit dog could be used to provide a blood transfusion for Crubie if necessary. Off they all went with Crubie, along with one of the collies used for working the sheep. There was no transfusion required but Catriona was very graphic on the telephone, describing the colour of the vomit from my dog in the car on the way home! This however, I was told, did not stop them from having a pub lunch on the way back! This same vet, George Rafferty, became well-known after the BBC television series *The Vet*, which was produced in later years. A book was published following the TV series called *Beyond the Surgery Door*.

The second drama which occurred while I was away involved my golden pheasant, Goldie. Golden pheasants are spectacular birds with very colourful plumage, which incorporates bright-red tail feathers. Before I left, I had been concerned about the safety of visitors because of Goldie's aggressive behaviour towards them. I was the only person who could get near Goldie; he would go out of his way to attack others. If he saw strangers he would charge at them, and if they went off in their cars he would run behind them, despite being perfectly capable of flying. It was a peculiar sight to see such a bird running fast after a vehicle, his small, beady eyes wild with aggression.

During a call from home I heard that Goldie had tried to attack a holiday visitor who was staying in one of the cottages. I told Euan to go ahead and shoot my golden pheasant. The following night I heard the next instalment. Apparently Euan had taken a shot at Goldie, but the bird had escaped and sat watching him closely from a high tree-branch. Goldie then swooped down in rage on Euan, who fired a second shot. The golden pheasant lay on the ground, and so Euan went off for a spade in order to bury him. When he returned, Goldie had vanished; he had probably only been stunned. He was then observed by Euan, up another tree, looking even angrier!

Goldie was still alive when I returned home and I gave him away to Penny Weir at Craig Dhu, because she had a large outside cage for birds. She also found Goldie vicious, but decided to allow him to roam freely, although he continued to chase cars. The irony was that one day as Penny was reversing her car she ran him over, killing him. So that was the end of Goldie, we thought. But a few weeks later I saw a golden pheasant in the drive at Glentruim. To my knowledge, there were no golden pheasants in the vicinity, so this made me wonder whether Goldie too had joined some of our past spirits, and come back to haunt us!

The journey back from the trade fair in Dortmund was not without incident. The car broke down on the outskirts of Hull and I had to call for assistance. Having once again been assured by this AA man that the car was in working order, I came to a halt on the motorway an hour later. This time I telephoned the AA company demanding a transporter to take me and my car back to Scotland. Because there were certain boundaries that the transporter drivers had to observe, when we came to the end of each boundary my car was taken off one lorry and placed onto another. By the time we got to Perth at midnight, I pleaded with the driver not to pass me on to the next person but to take me home, which I said was only about an hour up the road. He obliged, but over two hours later, having repeatedly asked me, 'How much further?' he could barely contain his frustration, eventually dumping me off at the caravan park around 2.30 a.m.

I worked hard to promote my tapestry business, and was soon contacted by a Japanese company which had become interested in my products. Their representatives came to visit me at

Glentruim to discuss marketing my kits in Japan. They also informed me that the packaging would have to be altered since, in their country, the wrapping reflected the gift, and should match the exquisiteness of its contents.

There then followed an invitation to London to take part in a programme on needlework for a Japanese television company. After several bobs and bows, I was led across a vast open-plan office at the top of a very smart, modern building. I was shown to a chair at the far end of the room where the television crew was waiting. My Japanese interviewer, from the London company, sat opposite me and, with very little English, commenced the interview. He struggled with the language as I did my best to answer his half-formulated questions. Eventually, when he was totally lost for words, I tried hard to make conversation myself, asking him how he and his colleagues enjoyed working in an open-plan environment. I had never seen an office such as this before and the layout intrigued me. His reply was, 'It is good, it is very sexual!' I knew that he meant 'social' and tried not to smile, but I could see the camera-man's arms shake up and down as he muffled his laughter. I was then taken to the most expensive Japanese restaurant in London, which was a great treat and a lovely end to an exciting day. Negotiation thereafter was drawn out, with much attention to detail, but as days ran into months it became too complicated to make a deal with that company.

I progressed from tapestries to fashion, having established by this time a small cottage industry that employed out-workers all over the Highlands. The business moved into tartan cotton and silk skirts, knickerbockers and shirts, with similar styles of clothes for children, to match those of the adults. Models wearing these garments were photographed in the gardens of Glentruim, and the pictures used for our advertising literature. This fashion side of the business was called Tapistyle, a mixture of tapestry and style, since some of the designs had fine embroidery incorporated into the cuffs and collars.

185

More trade fairs were planned, and one year Euan and I decided to attend Prêt-à-Porter in Paris, a well-known fashion trade fair. We stayed with our friend Eve Judlin and her family, at Saint Claud, outside Paris. As my mother had grown up with Eve's mother when she was at art school in Paris, we were thus into the second generation of friendship. We had to travel each day into the centre of Paris for the exhibition, which was patrolled by numerous policemen, who, because there had recently been a bomb scare, were making random car-checks. It was the same when we got to Prêt-à-Porter, where we were thoroughly searched on entry. The French officials, enjoying a joke, asked Euan, who was wearing his kilt, whether he should be searched with the ladies or the men!

Halfway through the week Euan became unwell, developing a temperature, which meant I found myself having to drive alone into Paris until he recovered. Circumnavigating the Arc de Triomphe with everyone hooting at everyone else was a new experience for me and took my full concentration. During Euan's indisposition, our Paris agent, Gillaine, did accompany me when available, but as she could not drive she was not much help to me. She amused us one winter, during a stay at Glentruim. We had planned to eat in the kitchen, which was warmer than the dining-room, and when it was time to leave the boudoir for our meal, she put on her fur coat!

Although Prêt-à-Porter had been successful for us, resulting in orders from many of the little boutiques in Paris, nevertheless we knew that much depended on our production when we returned home. To meet increased demand, we had garments made in a Perthshire factory supervised by Irene Thompson, the wife of one of my father's medical partners. The rag trade, we discovered, was a cut-throat business. Our products were no sooner on the market than a bigger, wealthier company would copy our designs, undercutting us. We did not have the capital to make our business grow at the speed necessary for survival, so, reluctantly and after much thought, we felt that we had to give it up. In retrospect, I felt that perhaps I should have persevered, but I hated sewing and I hated fashion. I never enjoyed shopping for clothes, nor did I understand why so many ladies felt that they should keep up with the current vogue. I could honestly say that my heart was never in that particular enterprise of ours!

# 23

# *The Cook Book*

EUAN and I sat together one autumn evening, discussing our dilemma. We were wealthy in property, with a fortune in antiques, but our cash-flow was dire. We both would have loved to send the children to private schools for their secondary education, but the possibility for this was becoming more and more unrealistic. Sending them away seemed to be the best solution, partly because we were so busy and could not give the children as much time as we would have liked, and partly because we felt, rightly or wrongly, that private secondary education was the best. The financial situation was so grim that Euan told me we would have to abandon the idea. After racking my brains, I came up with a potential solution.

'I know what we can do', I said with enthusiasm, 'I will write a cookbook'.

I had created numerous recipes with game and fish over the years, all of which had been enjoyed by those staying for fishing or shooting: it would be very satisfying to have them all written down, particularly if income could be generated in the process.

'It is easy to write a book,' replied Euan, in a tone that portrayed forthcoming doom. 'Anyone can write a book, but to get it published is another thing.' His words did not stop me. I ignored his fear of failure and rattled off my plan.

'I will write fourteen dinner menus for hostesses such as myself, who have to produce a different meal each night for their guests. Visitors do not usually stay more than two weeks, and thinking out the menus is the worst part of entertaining.'

I decided that the recipes would be named after different parts of the estate, with an anecdote preceding each one. I became used to the sad scene of Euan sitting by the fire, staring into the flames, pipe in one hand and whisky in the other. I knew what he was thinking: it would be disaster, the loss of Glentruim around the next corner.

My mind was made up. There would be no home-made Christmas presents that year, because I would be spending all my spare time on my cookbook. I got to work on it the next day. The family were subjected to game, fish, and more game at meal times. I placed my normal dollops of ingredients onto scales to be accurately weighed, with pencil in hand, and documented the details of every meal. This was the most difficult task of the book. There were times that I would be so tired after a busy day that I could not settle to write. On one such late afternoon I watched a programme on television about Barbara Cartland, who was talking about her novels. I admired her drive and was fascinated by her determination. It was during this programme that I received the best advice I could have wished for to enable me to complete my book. She said that what one should do every day was to start with the most important project; the housework and other commitments could wait. She qualified her statement by saying that one's mind would then be at peace to carry out everything else. I took this advice and, when I returned from taking the children to school, I would work on my book. Barbara Cartland was right: having spent a few hours writing, the daily duties fell into place. In the evening I would weigh ingredients, document amounts, and prepare the dinner which was to be described in the cookery book. The next day I would start again, writing up the previous evening's work. This was my pattern through the long winter, which meant that by the next Easter, 1983, I had my book finished. I called it *Dinners in a Scottish Castle*.

Although three publishers were interested, the book was successfully produced later in the year by Paul Harris, with colourful pictures taken by George Cocker. The back cover had a picture of Glentruim, with me standing in front of it in a ballgown and one of my peacocks sitting on the iron stairs leading to the drawing-room French doors. The front cover was taken behind the table in the dining-room, along with our piper, Mr Brough.

As planned, I had written a short anecdotal paragraph above each chapter, which tied in with the names of the dishes in each menu, such as the description of Craig Dhu being 'a steep mountain of grey, furrowed cliffs and wind-torn cloud, standing over Glentruim'. There were fifteen chapters (an extra day added to the two weeks!) of three-course meals with suggestions for vegetables and wines. At the back of the book I gave recipes using leftovers, followed by a few pages on 'final tips'.

In the introduction I described the way in which tradition took over at dinner parties. 'Before a dinner party all the guests assemble in the drawing-room, talking and laughing, with the distant, haunting sound of a piper playing the music of long ago in the hall outside. Some do not notice when the music stops, but then there is the heavy sound of the great gong summoning guests to the dining table. The sound of the pipes starts again and the piper entering the drawing-room silences all conversation.'

When I first came to live in my husband's home, I noted a curious tradition. As the piper walks through the room it is the privilege of the laird, as host, to choose the most attractive female guest and to offer her his arm as the piper leads them into the dining-room. It is, however, the privilege of his lady to choose the most attractive man to follow her husband, and the other male guests then follow with their own choice of partner. But they cannot choose, no matter how attractive, their own wives! In the dining-room, the piper proceeds down the whole length of the long table and up the other side. The laird, upon reaching his own place at the head of the table, stops and places his chosen lady on his right. In the same way the hostess, at the bottom of the table, stops and places her chosen partner on her left. Each gentleman then follows, holding the chair for his chosen partner.

It is a very old and curious tradition, how old I do not know, but because of it each person at the dining table finds themselves in company which they enjoy. It is, in my view, a far better way of seating guests than by trying to decide who would like to sit next to whom, and then rather arbitrarily allocating names to each place.

Those dinner parties I wrote about were extremely gracious. I remember at the close of dinner a message being passed from Euan's eyes to mine with a quiet smile. This signified thanks, and was also a hint that as hostess I should rise. As I rose, so did all the others, each gentleman holding back the chair of his partner. The ladies then retired to the drawing room, to leave the gentlemen alone. We talked quietly together, but our conversation was constantly interrupted by the laughter of the menfolk we had left behind in the dining room. There they sat with port and brandy, enjoying the wide, generous company of men together. Later they joined us, and again there was silence. The logs glowed and sparked in the white marble fireplace. My fingers at first would gently touch the strings of the clarsach, and then more confidently the chords rang out. In this way all the lovely Gaelic songs, many of them hundreds of years old, were revived and loved again.

Both children were ill with German measles when I had to proofread the cookbook before finally sending it to the publishers. Vivian Haddow, the wife of one of Euan's colleagues in Inverness, had done a superb job of typing out all my recipes, a labour of love in my opinion. It would have been so much easier in the new age of computers. I put both children in the same room for the time being and sat for hours by the window checking my text, but it turned out that I too was incubating this childhood disease; feeling like this everything became a struggle for me.

The previous time I had contracted an illness from the children was when I had mumps, which was unbelievably painful. This trauma was compounded by having to look after some sick sheep, which we were wintering for a farmer in the south of Scotland. Snow had covered the grass in the fields, and the sheep somehow managed to find their way into the policies. As the only green vegetation the sheep could see was the foliage of the yew trees in front of our house, hunger unfortunately enticed them to feed on it. The yew being poisonous to sheep, those which had eaten the leaves were taken severely ill. Cold tea was the necessary antidote, according to old wives' tales! I spent hours with ailing sheep up in the barns, although the most critically sick were housed in the butler's pantry. All were fed on cold tea out of a baby's bottle. The pain in my swollen glands was exacerbated by the severe chill as I fed each sick sheep every two hours. Only a few animals were lost; I was glad that I had managed to save the majority, especially since I felt so poorly.

The book was launched in Edinburgh at one of the bookshops, as well as at the Book Festival. The Clan Gathering that year provided me with a chance to sign copies, after which I also had to attend radio and television shows, undertaking cookery demonstrations all over Scotland and abroad.

Having written to Barbara Cartland and informed her how she had inspired me to complete my cookbook, I received a lovely letter back from her, with a signed copy of her own latest edition.

With success, you discover your true friends. I was saddened to find a couple of my so-called friends scathing about the book. 'Your book is a joke,' said one, 'I cannot believe you used margarine instead of butter!' At that time butter was frowned upon for health reasons, so I used margarine instead! Another did not like me using my Highland title, 'Lady Glentruim', although I had been encouraged to do so by none other than the Lord Lyon King of Arms. Indeed, he had told me that I should continue using the title so that it would not be forgotten by future generations.

It is a fallacy to think that writing a book makes money. It can make a little, but not the amount we required. You have to write a bestseller to make a fortune, and very few manage to do this. I did, however, make enough to keep the children at private schools, through the spin-offs.

I then began to experience a different kind of life within the cookery world, where I met famous chefs and cooks. My friends from the past could not believe what I was achieving. When I first married all I could cook was a boiled egg! Necessity had thrown me into experimenting with food, and I loved it. Euan used to tell everyone that I became a good cook only because of him. On tasting the first mouthful of one of my early efforts, he would often look up at me and ask, 'How did you make that?' Ignorant of cooking and never following any recipe books, I could only reply, 'I made it out of my head.' As he was the most severe critic of all my culinary endeavours, I greatly valued his honest opinion.

Catherine Brown, a Scottish food writer, was the first to approach me with a proposition. Having just finished yet another of her own cookery books, she had become involved with a company called *A Taste of Scotland*. At that time the organisation was run in conjunction with the Scottish Tourist Board, acting as a guide to establishments in Scotland which offered fresh produce and skilful cuisine. Colonel Pat Paterson was its chief executive. Catherine asked me if I would inspect hotels and restaurants in the Highlands and Islands, judging them on their overall performance in the process. I accepted, and this was the start of ten years with *A Taste of Scotland*.

Thereafter we combined our holidays with touring around Scotland, where I visited restaurants and hotels to inspect and write about them for the guide. This was how, from a very early age, our children learned about good food and good wines, providing them with a useful aspect of education for their future. I used to say to the children, 'You can only come with me if you eat the puddings.' I never had room for a sweet, but it was useful if I could have a taste of theirs. Sometimes, when they could not manage their second course I would remind them of our deal! On one famous occasion, during a stay at a very upmarket hotel near Wick in the far north of Scotland, I realised just how spoilt they were becoming. There were four-poster beds, en-suite bathrooms, and many other facilities in each room. The children were peeved because their room did not have a television and ours did! After an unsavoury scene, I told them that they must be the only children in Scotland lucky enough to travel around Scotland from one grand hotel to another and to enjoy the best food that Scotland had to offer.

When Rod Clerk, a clan member, organised a trip for me to go over to America to promote my book, Euan and I went together. After the comparative cool of Scotland, the intense heat when we arrived did not suit us. There was further annoyance when I found that many of the ingredients that I used for my recipes were unavailable. I had to take part in radio chatshows, and also one particular television show that I shall never forget. I had to prepare my dishes on a platform, with cooker and worktops, outside the studio; then, when it was my turn to be on, my whole platform was wheeled into the studio before a waiting audience. I worked away at my recipes and chatted about the ingredients and procedures. I had already made a large 'Prince's Crown', as I called it in my book. This was a skinned melon, with a Drambuie fruit jelly inside, decorated with cream and grapes on the outside. Moments before the cameras zoomed in on this creation, I saw a hand waving from below my stage. I then realised that a large bluebottle was trapped by its legs in the cream! The camera had already homed in and I had to face it. I talked through my recipe and without taking my eyes off the camera, surreptitiously used my finger to plunge the wriggling bluebottle deep into the cream. Fortunately I had said from the very start that the audience would not be able to taste my finished dishes for insurance reasons! Because of the heat, I knew that the food would in any case be inedible after the demonstration, particularly the fish dishes.

During this time, I was also asked to provide recipes for the Salmon Smokers Association, which was based in Aberdeen. I concocted recipe cards for their produce, which entailed travelling to Aberdeen for photograph shots of the menus. The association was asked to provide the recipes for a big function attended by the Princess Royal, and so I was obliged to contribute culinary ideas for this event too. I remember staying in Aberdeen for a couple of days producing the necessary meals, ready for photographs to be taken in a kitchen quite unknown to me, with equipment I had never tried before. It was not at all easy to work in such surroundings.

Later I was asked to produce recipes for 'Chunky Chicks', a chicken processing company outside Edinburgh. This was an experience in itself. I had not only to write recipe cards for the supermarkets, but also to deliver speeches in many of London's best hotels.

Ash Gupta was the Edinburgh PR company which arranged a visit to the United States on behalf of the Salmon Smokers' Association. I was to take my recipe cards and make speeches throughout New York, although I did not have to prepare any food dishes. The first event of my tour took place in Washington, at the Smithsonian Institute, opposite the White House. This was a vast and palatial venue for the occasion. There must have been thousands attending that night, when I talked about my life and about Scottish cuisine. The food offered to the guests was prepared according to my own recipes, carefully followed by the chefs in the building. It was a treat only to have to talk, without being required to make all the dishes. The cooks observed my instructions to perfection.

From there I travelled to Manhattan, where I had to deliver speeches on a boat as it sailed around the island. Of all the places I had been commissioned to work, Manhattan was my favourite because, aboard a boat, I was far away from the crowds and tall buildings.

Between these two events I had to return home for pressing business, but when I arrived back in New York I missed my chauffeured car at the airport. Taking a bus to Manhattan, I found myself in a most undesirable hotel and so had to change the following day to the extremely superior Temperance Hotel. This was well beyond my estimated budget; however, it was safe. The Tartan Exhibition was being held and I was also to be involved in this. I was invited to an ambassador's cocktail party, along with Nicolas and Sam Fairburn, as well as Lord Elgin, who also attended the Tartan Exhibition. It was a very jolly party and Lord Elgin sang beautifully at the piano. At this party I also met a charming man, David Farquharson OBE TD, who was in his seventies and had just been widowed. He asked me if I was alone in New York, to which I replied that I was. 'A woman alone – unheard of,' he said. 'I will come and escort you out to breakfast every day, and I will look after you.' He did just that, and I was most grateful, for I did not enjoy being on my own in New York. He also took me to a first night on Broadway. Since then we have corresponded every Christmas. New York was not a place to be on one's own and I hated being there without Euan.

I did brave the city by myself occasionally, but being a country person I was not cautious enough. Once I nearly had my bag stolen; I was constantly told by taxi drivers to keep my door locked. David told me to leave my gold bracelet in the hotel safe and not to wear designer clothes (of which I had none!). I was glad to return to the Highlands.

At the same party at which I had met David, I was also introduced to Cliff Robertson, whom I subsequently discovered was a famous actor, and we also kept in touch. One day he wrote to me at Glentruim, saying that as he was coming to a Robertson Clan Gathering to be held in the Atholl Palace Hotel in Pitlochry and he would like to take me out to dinner. I wrote back and said that since I had been asked to give a food demonstration that night at the Robertson Gathering, not only would I be delighted to see him, but would also like to invite him to stay at Glentruim. We met after my demonstration and went into the cocktail bar. Just as I was at the bar buying the second round of drinks before dinner, I was approached by an old friend of mine, Laurence Blair-Oliphant, with whom I had grown up. He asked me how I knew Cliff Robertson. I told him how Cliff and I had met and he seemed very interested. He then added, 'How exciting to know such a talented actor!' I rejoined Cliff and asked him if he was indeed an actor. I then discovered all the films that he had starred in, *Wells Fargo* being one of the first to make him famous. Needless to say, I was impressed!

For years I carried out demonstrations for various companies and for charities, also writing for magazines on the subject of Scottish food. I worked with *A Taste of Scotland* and was ultimately asked by Jack MacMillan, the new Chief Executive, to be their chief inspector, a post which I accepted. During my time with them there were numerous amusing incidents, the tales of which have yet to be told. It was also very satisfying for me to know that on the proceeds of all of this activity the children's school fees were paid.

# 24

# *The Shooting Parties*

ALTHOUGH catering for shooting parties was tiring, I also took pleasure in it when those who came were of a certain distinction. The arrival of European royalty caused a great stir in our household, and I spent many days in preparation for one such royal visit. The prince had to have his own room with an adjoining bathroom, as did his princess. The rooms which had been allocated to them had been redecorated, new curtains had been commissioned, and their beds were made with crisp new linen. Scallops and lobster were flown over from Stornaway, but all of the game came from the Glentruim estate. An old school friend of mine in Stornaway, Margaret Engebretsen, organised the purchase of the shellfish for me, with the consignment sent by bus from Inverness airport. The shellfish were alive when delivered to MacRae's grocery shop in Newtonmore for us to collect. They had been packed in large boxes, the lobsters' claws secured by rubber bands. I had never seen such large scallops before: they were exquisite. There would indeed be a feast fit for a king!

While the royal party was out shooting grouse over Glentruim, I drove the Land Rover, the back full of a lunchtime spread, to Shepherds' Cottage. It was a warm summer's day, the windows of the Land Rover were wide open and the sweet scent of birch filled the air. I was hot with the sun, and also from the exertion of preparing the picnic at great speed. I motored up the back drive past the Piper's Cottage, the Keeper's and Kennel Cottages by the pond, and then up past the Home Farm. When I reached the back road I turned towards Laggan, where, not far away on my right, set in the dyke of the wall closest to the road, was the stone to which I often guided visitors. This stone has a cross on it and is believed to mark the centre of the Highlands. Then as I turned the next corner, I looked down to the east of the Glentruim mansion, over Shanvall, which used to be part of a settlement of seven houses and barns. The largest outcrop had been a former school, which was attended by pupils from as far away as Laggan. This idyllic place, from which the views stretched up and down the valley and across to Craig Dhu, was where Euan and I had always planned to live in our old age, once Glentruim house became too large for us.

In 1954, long before we came to Glentruim, Aunt Katie had let Shanvall to James and Cecile Macpherson. They were not related to the Glentruim Macphersons, but were close clan members. James had been in banking in Borneo before he retired, and we could understand why he chose Shanvall for his retirement. James and Cecile were given a twenty-five year lease on the property, which was later extended for another ten years. When they first took over the cottage it had earth floors, no roof, no running water and no electricity. The living area and bedrooms were upstairs, below which was merely an animal shelter with a mud floor. A great deal of restoration had therefore been required before these tenants could make the cottage habitable. James and Cecile did not have electricity installed, which meant that the days of open fires and candle-light lingered on for them. In 1968 James died and his younger son, Colin, inherited the tenancy until around 1980, when the lease expired and Shanvall came back into the Glentruim estate.

Leaving Shanvall behind me, a short distance further on I came to what we called the Crooked Bridge, which was near a sharp bend in the road. Long ago there was an old rowan tree there, where bees used to swarm and honey could be gathered, if you knew where to look. This spot, beside the bridge, was well-known for sightings of a ghostly white lady. When the moon was full, nobody would pass this place; even horses would shy away and ford the river further down. Dogs howled mournfully at what they could see, but which their owners could not. The story that used to be told was that a curious local took a bet with his friend to cross this bridge. His horse stopped short of the bridge, so he himself crossed it on foot, only to witness the white lady, with outstretched arms, who appeared at the base of the rock. What happened next was never known, but the local gentleman was found the next day, face down in a pool of water. The white lady was later seen again by another person from the village. He had visited the place at full moon, when the rock was lit up by a brilliant white light – and he saw the lady, her arms held out before her as if beckoning to him. He returned home safely that night, but was terrified by his experience for a long time afterwards.

Further along the road, to my left, I looked up over the purple hills of Glentruim etched against the brilliant blue sky, and to the right I looked down across the rich green fields, sloping towards the upper Spey valley. I heard gunshots, then the call of a pheasant, which had been startled by the echo of gunfire through the valley. By that time I was in sight of Shepherds' Cottage at the foot of the hill.

Before I unloaded the back of the Land Rover, I unlocked the door and entered. The cottage had been kept cool by its thick stone walls, so after lighting the fires to give cheer, rather than warmth, I then brought in the food. A cold salmon, chicken and beef were laid out on the table, with salads and freshly-baked brown bread, which I had recently taken out of the oven. The smell of the yeast from the bread and peat from the fires would be enticing for the arrival of the party off the hill.

I looked up at the Crags of Glentruim to the summit of the hill and remembered an unfortunate time when I had gone up there with Douglas Weir. Doug, who was very knowledgeable about wildlife and also a great artist, had told me that I must go and see the nest of peregrine falcons which he had spotted over the edge of a crag. We had taken most of the morning to get up there, and I was excited at the thought of seeing the peregrine chicks. Doug had gone before me, and as he lay stretched out over the edge of the rock to look down on the nest, he was thrilled to find them as easily as he had before. Then it was my turn. I got within about three feet of the rock face and started to tremble. Doug told me I would be quite safe and that he would hold on to my feet. But I could not do it. I felt my head beginning to spin and my mouth went dry with fear. After much persuasion, I reluctantly did as I was told, but my anxiety was very apparent and I was ashamed of myself for being so frightened. As we made our way down the hill, I explained to Doug the incident which had instigated my fear of heights. It had been when Euan had taken me on my first and last rock-climb, in the Lake District. Euan and a climbing friend had decided to take their new wives on a 'mild' rock-climb. His friend's wife, like me, had never been rock-climbing before. Euan was leading and, roped together, the four of us climbed the Middle Fell Buttress. I avoided looking down, and regretted agreeing to such a venture the moment I found no foot-holds. Euan had not been on this climb for many years and had lost his way, thus we climbed a 'severe' rock face instead of a 'mild' one. I hung over the rocks on the rope, heavy and limp with terror, as Euan hauled me up to the top like a sack of potatoes. The other wife followed suit and then, stricken with uncontrollable shaking, we both abandoned our men and walked back to the nearest pub. That was when I first developed a tremendous fear of heights, which has been with me ever since that day.

When I heard the motor of the Gnat, I knew that the shooting party was approaching. The Gnat was a sizeable three-wheeled vehicle which we often used for bringing the deer down from the

201

hill. It had one large wheel in front and two at the back. There was a round metal bar to steer with, two low seats, and a handy platform to the rear. The children used to have great fun around the bottom gardens on this machine! Euan and the prince arrived on the Gnat, the others in the party arriving soon after them. Everyone was offered champagne, but water and beer had to be the first drink for them to quench their thirst from fatigue and the heat of the day.

John Moneagle and his wife worked for us at Glentruim and John took many of our guests out shooting. He reminded me of the day he had been stalking stags up on the plateau above the grouse moor. He had spotted a huge pair of antlers, but nothing else of the stag could be seen, so he knew that it was lying down. Strangely enough, this stag was lying about a mile away from the rest of the herd. John crept in and got very wet crawling along the side of the burn. When he thought he was close enough, he whistled in order to startle the stag so that it would stand. He had to whistle a second time to make the stag move, and then he took a shot. After retrieving the deer, he noticed a huge gash in its side. Determined to find out what had caused this, he had gone back over the hill a couple of days later. He guessed what might have happened as he watched an enormous switch (deer with a single horn), stabbing another deer in the neck.

John had told me that, on another occasion, he had been totally embarrassed when he had come home with a deer shot by one of the German hunters. They had walked up through the woods to the top of Glentruim hill and had heard a stag, 'bellowing away something rotten,' as he described it. They had seen a very big stag about 200 metres below, so they had crawled on their stomachs to get a little closer. John had then told the guest to, 'Take this old fella, he's going back a bit [past his prime!], take your time and don't let him see or hear you. Wait till he turns.' The shot was fired and the beast dropped. 'Well done,' John praised the proud hunter. John gralloched (removed the entrails) of the deer, but he was perplexed to find no bullet-hole. After his return to Glentruim, he hung the deer up on the pulley in the garage, and immediately skinned and cleaned it. It was at this stage that he was able to give the carcass a thorough examination to search for the bullet-hole. Having found the track of the bullet, he shuddered to think what Euan would say at this unorthodox shot. But Euan could not stop laughing when John told him that the track of the bullet had gone in right up the 'eye of despair'! 'The what?' I asked. 'The arse!' John replied, breaking into fits of laughter. I suppose that there was no polite way of saying it!

The German hunters came for trophies, the bigger the better. Once they had shot their roe buck or stag, we had to boil the heads in the back yard of Glentruim. This was to take off every morsel of flesh, so that our visitors could take their trophies home with them, clean and white. Every aspect of hunting was important to them. There were tunes played on the German hunting-horn before they started their stalk, when they had killed their beast, and when they returned with their prize! It was also not unusual for them to make soup with the water from the boiled heads; I believe the deer's tongue was considered a delicacy. I drew the line when asked to make this soup. The smell outside, from the pot of boiling heads, was quite bad enough!

I had never wanted to kill an animal, but I had always thought that I should experience a stalk, just once in my life. Early one evening, Angie, our gamekeeper at the time, and I went after marauding stags. We had hoped to shoot a deer at the foot of the Glentruim hills before it crossed the road and went down into the bottom fields. We made our way along the road and, just in front of the woods, we saw a herd of deer walking down to the fence from the summit of the hill. Angie had instructed me how to hold the rifle and I had already had many practice shots on a target back at the house. I was told which stag to go for then

Angie lined me up and said, 'Fire!' I was so excited at seeing this beautiful creature through the scope that I forgot to press the butt of the rifle into my right shoulder and therefore, when I fired, the recoil forced the scope backwards, splitting open my forehead above my right eye. I had never known Angie as silent as when we drove home unsuccessful. He was very disappointed in me! When I arrived back at Glentruim, with blood running down my face, I went straight to the butler's pantry to wash in cold water. As I was cleaning up, the front door bell rang and Angie called for me to come. It was the police. We had been troubled with poachers and the police had come to investigate the shot, which they had heard while patrolling the area. I had to go to the door looking an awful sight, with blood and tinges of black and blue appearing on my face. 'Och, it was you, madam!' a police officer said, 'Well that's alright!' Well, it wasn't alright, because I had to drive Angie home to the village, still in total silence; he even lent me his sunglasses so that nobody would notice my bruised face. I was a sight, even with my cap pulled over my forehead. The next day my head was very swollen and I had a huge black eye, with shades of blue and purple creeping down my face. It took several weeks to heal completely.

Euan was a better shot than anyone, and our guests were impressed by his skills, as were those who worked for us. One night, when marauding deer were in the bottom fields below the terraced lawns at Glentruim, Euan and the gamekeeper went walking together quietly over the lawns and into the long grass at the other side. They then went over the burn in the woods, which had to be crossed before reaching the fields. Shooting using his .270 rifle, Euan fired five shots in a row: five stags went down. The next rifle was passed to him and, reloading, Euan fired again – the sixth stag fell. 'A night never to forget', I was told later.

Helga Klein and her husband once came to stay for a week, to shoot roe deer. Helga was petite, attractive and wore the latest fashions from her boutique in Munich. Her clothes were always beautiful, and she would come down to dinner in an exquisite gown every evening.

You can imagine the surprise of the gamekeeper when one morning, expecting the gentleman to rise early for the roe stalking, he instead found Helga waiting in the hall. She was wearing a green jacket, green plus-twos, a green German stalking hat with a feather in it, her bugle slung over her shoulder. Stepping outside with her stalker for the day, she proceeded to play a hunting tune. Home from the hunt, having gained her trophy, Helga then joined her husband in the dining room for breakfast. Before she started to eat, she would always ask if there had been any left-over dessert from the night before. This would then constitute her breakfast!

Once Helga and I had become great friends, at Christmas large boxes of designer clothes would arrive from Munich as gifts for me. These would be garments from her shop which had not sold in the season's sale!

When it came time to burn heather on the hill, two or three people were generally required for the task; these usually included Euan, the gamekeeper and one other volunteer. There was, however, a certain occasion when only Euan and the gamekeeper were available. There had been a particularly hot spell, which had desiccated the heather so completely that no encouragement was necessary for flames to take off and spread further than intended. The fire got so out of control that they both had to spend hours beating at the flames to put them out. Euan was overcome by the thick, dense smoke that followed. The gamekeeper came back to the house for assistance, but later, after they all finally returned with Euan, I had to call an ambulance. It was an hour's journey from Glentruim up to Raigmore Hospital in Inverness. Euan was cyanosed and very ill. However, there were definite signs of recovery when Euan asked me to bring in a dram and his pipe during visiting hours later that evening. I took his pipe, but not the whisky. Instead of the latter, I made a large

Bloody Mary (vodka and tomato juice), and poured it into a glass bottle, labelling it 'home-made tomato juice'! During one hospital visit I looked at the bottle containing my concoction, and, having thought that I had only filled it three-quarters of the way, was surprised to see it full to the top. Only later did I discover that Catriona, who was then about seven years old, had remembered her father saying that I never put enough vodka in a Bloody Mary. Noting the gap, she had filled it up with more vodka!

At the Raigmore Hospital, Euan had a private room with its own bathroom. Perhaps his laced tomato juice did indeed go unnoticed by the staff, but surely the smoke rising from beneath the bathroom door must have been a give-away?

Having totally recovered, Euan was soon back on the hill again, sometimes taking guests out shooting, and at other times burning heather, or even just walking with his dog for the pleasure of looking over Glentruim.

After the visit of every sporting guest, however, there would be a hunting tale, either to be remembered or else better forgotten. It was, however, the professionalism of Euan and the keepers, who naturally played an important role at Glentruim, which made every shoot unique for even the most unskilled huntsman.

# 25

# *Brigadoon*

BY the look on Euan's face, and listening to his side of the telephone conversation, I knew that he was excited about what he was hearing. It was an old friend of his, Ian Dean, who was speaking to him, and what he was telling him was almost too good to be true. An entrepreneur from America had asked Ian to find a location in Scotland for the remake of the film *Brigadoon*. But, this was not all; the village that was to be built for the film was to remain and be the backdrop for Scottish industry in the future. The idea was that, after the making of the film, each little cottage, built in the style of around 1700, would be a craft shop, advertising and selling its wares. Tweeds, kilts, whisky, bagpipes and fiddles were only a few of the products suggested. There was also to be a smithy, along with other tradesmen's cottages, in the village square, and a little church at the top of the hill. These plans were proposed during the summer of 1982, and the American was called Reeve Whitson.

After numerous lengthy telephone calls from the States, Reeve came to stay at Glentruim. He was tall, dark, never looked you in the eye, and had a distant presence about him. What impressed us most was that he seemed to know everyone who was worth knowing, and spoke about them as if they were old, close friends. The first name dropped was that of Art Linklater, who had supposedly been caught up in Reeve's enthusiasm over this innovative project, as were Allan Jay Lerner and his wife, Liz

Robertson, who were currently creating the new production of *My Fair Lady*. The list of very well-known characters, whom Reeve purported to have already approached, and who had apparently gone along with his idea, was endless, thus giving the whole project credibility.

The appointed architect was Professor Jimmy Paul from Dundee, who drew up intricate plans of the village, later coming to meet us during Reeve's first visit to Glentruim. Jimmy was originally from the east coast of Scotland: a fine-looking man, with his hair tied back in a pony-tail, which was as white as his long, shaggy beard. We soon applied for outline planning for the village that was to be built in the fields above Glentruim. It caused a buzz in the area, and the local inhabitants watched eagerly for progress, hoping that the film would generate income for them too. It was intended that the cottage industries would keep the area vibrant, far outliving the relatively short time taken for making a film.

We were at the end of the second year, no further forward with this project, as I sat in the boudoir with Euan, going over the 'Reeve Whitson Saga'. Reeve had been backwards and forwards to Glentruim, staying for weeks on end, our lives now totally taken over by *Brigadoon*. It was all becoming a great concern, particularly since no costs had been met, and Euan and I were becoming anxious about finances.

The first time Reeve had arrived at Glentruim, he had changed into his black tracksuit, the only garment I ever saw him dressed in, apart from a black suit and a black poloneck worn, only for meetings. When I showed him to his room, I had thought that his luggage was very minimal for someone staying for a few weeks. But Kathleen Maive and her grandmother, who accompanied Reeve, more than made up for his sparse wardrobe. Kathleen was an Irish dancer, world-class, a beautiful girl with thick, long, curly red hair and lovely long legs. As soon as you saw her dance, you knew why she had been chosen for the film.

After their arrival, Kathleen and her grandmother stayed in their bedrooms, but Reeve returned to the drawing room and immediately asked if he could use our telephone. Commandeering our telephone became a frequent habit of Reeve's, particularly during the night, when he called America. About an hour later, when joining us again, Reeve paced the floor as he spoke, veering from one subject to another whilst he included more names of famous people. His diatribe was almost impossible to absorb, and I began to wonder where the film came in all of this. Then, as if his thoughts took over his words, Reeve launched into plans for the film.

'It will be the ultra-modern rock situation, portraying the huge contrast of idealistic Brigadoon and modern America.' He had lost me from the start! 'Art Linklater, the director, is with us. Loewe will compose the music, Allan Lerner will produce the lyrics, and Liz Robertson, his wife, will sing,' Reeve rambled on. 'Of course, there are two more films, one about a monster. I have John Irvine lined up to direct this one, the other is Indianapolis 500. By the way,' he hastily added, 'you will meet Russ Ives when he comes to stay this week; he is our computer expert and was the key man for the special effects in *ET*; George Duffuss and Billy Connolly have also been approached.' Before I could ask where they came into all of this, Reeve was talking about the next few weeks of auditions. I could not keep up with his continual change of subject, and hoped that Euan had got the gist of it.

'Tomorrow, we are meeting Bob Cowan, the chairman of the Highlands and Islands Development Board: I met up with the Bank of Scotland yesterday, they are behind us, but I still have to get hold of Allan Shieach, of The Macallan Whisky,' Reeve continued. 'Allan is also with Scottish Screen productions in Glasgow.'

Reeve did not drive, which meant I had to take him to Inverness the next day for his appointment. Moreover, on the way home, he announced that there would be twelve people arriving for dinner, and eight for breakfast the next morning! Almost jamming on the brakes with fury, I asked who he thought was preparing the evening meal that was to be served in a couple of hours!

'Just give them cold cuts.' He had all the answers.

'What cold cuts?' I could hardly contain my anger as I diverted to the next village for provisions.

This became the pattern of our days with Reeve: no consideration, no warning regarding meetings, visitors, or about auditions that were to be held in the drawing-room. Musicians would come by train, plane or even helicopter and always had to be met.

John Moneagle, world-champion drummer, who had already been working for us, acted as chauffeur to Reeve when I was busy or unavailable. In the early hours of one morning, at Reeve's request, John arrived in his car to take him to the railway station. Jimmy Paul was also staying with us and we were all up late, talking about *Brigadoon*.

'Where on earth have they gone at this hour?' Euan asked Jimmy, as he looked at his watch.

'They've gone to the train to pick up two musicians and an Irish baritone for their auditions,' was the answer.

Saying not a word, Euan stood up, walked out of the room, then we could hear him locking and bolting the front doors. Back in the room, master of his own house, he told us to go to bed, and he then proceeded to turn off all the lights behind us.

We ignored the ringing of the front door bell when they returned from the station. A little later we heard music wafting down from the barn, up at the old Home Farm. The auditions were obviously taking place there, even at that unsociable hour!

Reeve contacted the top directors of the most élite companies in Scotland, Harris Tweed and Loch Carron being two of the cloth manufacturers. Alistair Buchan from Loch Carron, which produces tartan cloth and kilts, soon became a frequent participant in telephone discussions between himself and us. 'Is this man for real?' we would say to each other, all praying that *Brigadoon* would happen.

Alistair and his wife had come across Reeve while they were in America, and were introduced to well-respected and known individuals, who were also caught up in Reeve's vision.

'We were introduced to Art Linklater, and we were also given tickets for a show by Reeve, where, during the interval, we met Andrew Lloyd Webber and Sarah Brightman backstage in their dressing room,' Alistair told me. 'Everyone we talked to was waiting for *Brigadoon* to get past the "idea" stage! We even attended one of the Highland Games and watched Kathleen dance.'

I was then reminded by Jimmy that at home in Scotland, Reeve had been in touch with John Burgess, a champion piper, Ron Gonnella, a world-famous fiddler, and Donny McLeod, a Gaelic folk singer, who also presented children's programmes in Gaelic. According to Alistair, there had also been contact with John Currie, a music and ballet director from Perth! I also learnt that little Martyn Bennett was Reeve's 'star child of tomorrow' on the pipes, and Billy Forsyth, dancer, was another top artist to be included. He had chosen the cream of the entertainment world in Scotland. He said that he had picked Glentruim because it was unique, hidden away right in the centre of the Highlands, as marked on the Ordnance Survey map, and also because this land belonged to one of the oldest families in Scotland.

Even Jimmy had bizarre tales to tell. When he visited Reeve in America, he had been taken to San Diego to watch 'pilotless' planes, as they were described. Then later Reeve told him there was an exciting new project involving racing cars, outside London! Jimmy was also given the impression that a film was to be made about Skortzeny, one of Hitler's men. Jimmy had actually met Skortzeny's wife on several occasions, during and after the days of Reeve.

The whole affair was shrouded in mystery; Reeve's idea never did transform into reality. We had wined and dined countless people for Reeve, listened to auditions, organised ceilidhs and attended numerous meetings. We felt tired, used and, worst of all, had received no kind of financial reimbursement for either our expenses or our time.

Having had enough of the whole affair, yet bemused by it all, my mistrust took me to Reeve's room one afternoon when he was out. I was desperate to make sense of it all as I stood over his small luggage bag, but all I could see was one change of clothes and a little notebook which, uncharacteristically, I opened. None of his scribbling made sense to me, being in note-form and distinctly disjointed, just like his verbal communication. The words reflected a stream of consciousness – so many ideas, but nothing that could indicate a 'deal' of any kind.

I discussed my findings with Euan, and we decided to ask Robert Turcan, an old friend and lawyer in Edinburgh, to confront Reeve on our behalf. We all sat in the smoking-room, the atmosphere so laden with tension that I was reminded of my first encounter with that historic room, during the reading of the will. Euan and I sat on the couch together, Robert in an armchair. Reeve was offered a chair, but chose to hover. Reeve listened to the ultimatum given by Robert, then left immediately. He had gone out of our lives forever, taking Kathleen and the grandmother with him. Their departure was so sudden that they left their luggage for me to ship back to America.

All those who had any sort of dealings with Reeve Whitson had been well and truly conned. Because he had persuaded so many respected people in high positions to be part of his scheme, his proposed venture had gained more than a gloss of credibility. Reeve, we discovered, was a clever man; it was said that he was once in the Special Services and had worked with Bruce Lee, the top exponent of Kung Fu. Also, it was even thought that Reeve had been Eisenhower's bodyguard! He certainly knew how to play one person along with the other.

Louise Batchelor, from BBC television, had meanwhile been reporting on the development of the *Brigadoon* project on the evening news. When it all came to an end, she came to Glentruim with Kirsty Wark to interview us. A series of special features were run on the evening news, culminating in a live television interview with Reeve in the States. His bluff had finally been called.

Reeve would never allow his photograph to be taken, and had no cheque book, but only wads of cash in his pocket. His identity was dubious: indeed I heard someone describe him as a 'non-person'. He worked on the confident assumption that his recruited dignitaries were impressed by each other. As a result, all were resolute in being part of this fictitious production of *Brigadoon*. But nothing could have been further from the idealistic dream.

And so the struggle to keep Glentruim was to continue. Our hopes of the most promising business had been dashed. We had made numerous sacrifices, not least the times which separated us from our children; without a doubt we all suffered because of this. However, life goes on and one makes the best of things, doing what seems to be right for all concerned. I can only hope that our children have managed to put their thoughts of past days at Glentruim into perspective, above all treasuring the good memories and forgetting the bad.

# *Epilogue*

I began my life at Glentruim in the smoking-room, and my last story ends in it. I arrived young, full of hope and promise for our future, determined to keep our heritage in the family for the sake of generations to come. No matter what happens in the following years, at least I will know that I have done my utmost to save Glentruim, have been enriched by my experience, and have no regrets. Furthermore, my boundless energy will keep me focused on the next challenge that comes my way. As always, I will work tirelessly, striving to succeed.

Over the turbulent years at Glentruim, there was happiness and sadness; there are stories yet to be told, and stories that will never be told. It was the hand of Lachlan, Euan's grandfather, that rocked the cradle, and he later led the infant in it, Grace, through a fulfilling and fruitful life, just as Euan led me into maturity, encouraged me, and taught me the things that mattered desperately. The difference in our ages was meaningless, since there is no such thing as time when two lives are bonded together.

This 'Strange Wild Place' called Glentruim, which in 1844 Lord Coburn doubted was habitable, depending as it did entirely on the trees coaxed into life to protect it, has now witnessed the growth of sturdy plantations. It has also been blessed by the extension of our family line, and I would dearly like to think that our future generations will be as vigorous as the forests that surround Glentruim. Indeed, Euan used to say to me that when you have children, through them you have immortality. I firmly believe that the spirits of our ancestors are with me, and that they will continue to stretch out a hand to guide me now, and when most in need. After all, I am now part of Glentruim.

# References

*The Buildings of Scotland: Highlands and Islands* by John Gifford: published by Penguin Books

*In the Glens Where I was Young by Meta Humphrey Scartlett:* published by Siskin Milton of Moy

*Laggan's Legacy: A Personal History of a Highland Community by its People:* printed by Redwood Books

*The Legend of the Cairngorms* by Affleck Gray: published by Mainstream Publishing

*The Poetry of Badenoch* by The Reverend Thomas Sinton: published by The Northern Counties Publishing Company Ltd

*Queen Victoria's Highland Journals*, edited by David Duff: published by Webb and Bower

*The Wild Braes: Book in the Glens Where I was Young by Meta Humphrey Scarlett:* published by Fiskin